Study Speaking

ENGLISH FOR ACADEMIC PURPOSES titles from Cambridge

Study Skills in English *by Michael J. Wallace*

Study Listening – Understanding lectures and talks in English
by Tony Lynch

Study Writing – A course in written English for academic and
professional purposes *by Liz Hamp-Lyons and Ben Heasley*

Study Reading – A course in reading skills for academic purposes
by Eric H. Glendinning and Beverly Holmström

Study Speaking – A course in spoken English for academic purposes
by Tony Lynch and Kenneth Anderson

Study Speaking

A course in spoken English for academic purposes

Tony Lynch
Kenneth Anderson
Institute for Applied Language Studies, University of Edinburgh

CAMBRIDGE
UNIVERSITY PRESS

Published by the Press Syndicate of the University of Cambridge
The Pitt Building, Trumpington Street, Cambridge CB2 1RP
40 West 20th Street, New York, NY 10011–4211, USA
10 Stamford Road, Oakleigh, Victoria 3166, Australia

© Cambridge University Press 1992

First published 1992
Reprinted 1992

Printed in Great Britain
at the Bath Press, Avon

A catalogue record for this book is
available from the British Library.

ISBN 0 521 39551 8 Book
ISBN 0 521 42599 9 Cassette

Contents

Student's materials

Resource materials

Teacher's guide

Acknowledgements

We would like first to thank the students and teachers at the Institute for Applied Language Studies (IALS) of the University of Edinburgh, whose comments on several generations of classroom materials have helped to shape this book. We should mention (in chronological order) Carole Franklin, Cathy Benson, Jane Palfery, David Hill, Mary Ann Julian, Esther Daborn, Anne Heller, Eric Glendinning, Hugh Trappes-Lomax, Ron Howard, Neil Jones, Jennifer Higham, Lilias Davies and Jill Northcott.

We also benefited from the feedback provided by teachers in various countries who used the pilot version of *Study Speaking* with their EAP learners. Some of the additions to (and many omissions from!) the final version are the direct result of their comments and criticisms. In particular, we are grateful to Bernard Coffey and Guy Netley of the University of Reading and Barbara Cornish of the British Council English Language Centre, Jakarta, for suggestions that we have incorporated into the book.

The project would not have been completed without the encouragement and expertise of Peter Donovan, Annemarie Young, Elizabeth Serocold and Alison Silver of Cambridge University Press at different stages of the project, and the cooperation of Clive Criper and Eric Glendinning, Directors of IALS, in allowing us the time to write and revise the materials.

Finally, our thanks go to everyone who took part in the recordings featured in the pilot and final versions: Mihai Ciucu, Sheena Davies, Eileen Dwyer, Julia Feng Whittome, Mauro Franzoni, Nathalie Louppe, Faris Al-Naemi, Jill Northcott, Endang Parwati, Tom Tatsumi, Hugh Trappes-Lomax and Elspeth Wardrop.

Thanks to Ilanit Cohen, Pemica Chinvong, Naomi Makino, Bareno Karim, Yves Yesse, Jihwan Chang and Kristina Buchholz for appearing on the cover.

The table on pages 34, 45 and 85 from the *Annual Abstract of Statistics 1989* is reproduced by permission of HMSO.
Drawings by Peter Brown. Artwork by Wenham Arts.
Book designed by Peter Ducker MSTD.

'I guess I should warn you: if I turn out to be particularly clear, you've probably misunderstood what I said.'

Alan Greenspan, Chairman of the US Federal Reserve

Course map

Unit/Theme	Phase 1: Information task	Phase 2: Scenario	Phase 3: Seminar skills Presentation	Participation
1 Starting a course	Course structure	Bank	Signposting	
2 University systems	Student societies	Library	Delivery	
3 Accommo-dation	Layout of a flat	Accommo-dation office	Using visual aids	
4 Language	Language learning	Language courses		Getting clarification
5 Teaching	Departmental organisation	Postponing an essay		Questioning
6 Health	Medical treatment	Doctor's surgery	Non-verbal signals	
7 Evaluation	Travel grant committee	Examination results	Concluding	
8 Research	Research trends	Research proposal		Disagreeing

Extension work: Individual seminars

Suggestions for further action

To the student

Who is the course for?

Study Speaking has been written for people who need to speak English in connection with their academic work. It is intended in particular for use on language programmes preparing learners of English for work and study in an English-speaking context.

What does the course cover?

If you look at the *Course map* on the opposite page, you will see that there are eight units, each on an overall theme relevant to people approaching a course of study through English: the way courses are organised and taught, finding suitable accommodation, getting medical treatment, academic assessment, and so on.

Each unit is divided into three Phases, which cover different aspects of successful speaking:

1. **Information tasks** concentrate on improving the *clarity* with which you communicate facts and concepts; the activities involve solving problems based on verbal and graphic input.

2. **Scenarios** focus on the *flexibility* with which you react in situations where you need to persuade someone to accept your view.

3. **Seminar skills** work sharpens the *effectiveness* of your contributions to seminars and formal discussions, whether as a main speaker or as a member of the audience. The work involves analysing and practising skills of presentation and participation, through mini-seminars in small groups. The final part of the course, **Extension work**, provides practice in longer seminars (main presentation, discussion and teacher comment).

How does the course work?

All the speaking tasks involve three elements: preparation, performance and feedback. They have been designed to make you *think* as well as speak and listen. Becoming a more effective communicator is not simply a matter of practising the spoken language; practice certainly helps, but the real improvements come from planning *how* to approach a speaking task and evaluating *how well* you spoke.

1

In short, the book aims to help you to *study* speaking – by thinking about what is required in a specific situation, trying out what you have planned, and then analysing alternative ways of achieving your speaking goal.

To the teacher

Aims

Study Speaking has been written with the following aims:
1. to activate and extend the learners' linguistic competence;
2. to increase their confidence in using spoken English;
3. to develop their ability to analyse and evaluate spoken performance;
4. to sharpen their strategic competence in face-to-face interaction.

The book has been designed to push the learners to produce the 'comprehensible output' that Swain (1985) has argued is an essential component in progress in a foreign language. The tasks provide springboards to (inter)action by challenging their intellectual and linguistic resources. Having tried out a solution to a particular communicative problem, they are helped to analyse how well they coped and to discuss alternative strategies.

Our intention is that as a result of using this course, language learners should realise that there is usually more than one possible route to any communication goal and that success can depend as much on knowing how to approach a problem as on knowing what to say. The course therefore aims to improve the *quality* of their speaking skills as well as to increase the *quantity* of their knowledge of the language system.

We attach particular importance to getting learners to evaluate their own performances, rather than to rely solely on assessment and correction from the teacher. Studies of the role of consciousness-raising (e.g. Sharwood Smith, 1981; Rutherford, 1987) suggest that as long as the teacher retains the dominant role in evaluating classroom performance, students may not engage in the sort of active self-monitoring that may lead to conscious decisions to change target language behaviour.

Rationale

In writing *Study Speaking* we have been influenced by the findings of research into the relationship between classroom communication practice and overall progress in the foreign language. These could be summarised as follows:

1. Learning a foreign language requires access to comprehensible input (Krashen, 1981). In conversation 'difficult' input may be made comprehensible through the mutual efforts of the participants to make appropriate adjustments to the interaction. Skill in making such

adjustments forms part of 'strategic competence' in the language (Canale and Swain, 1980).

2. It follows from (1) that it is not only inevitable but necessary for the learner to encounter comprehension problems in order to make progress by solving them. Conversation offers the potential for the development of knowledge of and about the target language, and also of skills in problem solving (Faerch and Kasper, 1986).

3. Classroom tasks differ in the linguistic and strategic demands they make of learners. Those that require two-way information exchange result in more interactional adjustment (Doughty and Pica, 1986) than those in which such exchange is optional. On 'divergent' tasks – where learners do not share a common goal, e.g. a debate on a controversial issue – students tend to produce fewer but longer speaking turns than on 'convergent' tasks such as information-gap activities (Duff, 1986). Courses in spoken language should provide a balanced diet of both types of task.

4. A learner's use of interactional strategies should be judged by the effectiveness in getting the message conveyed, rather than by the accuracy of their form (Tarone and Yule, 1989); the components of strategic competence should be the explicit focus of classroom practice, and not regarded as something that will naturally develop with increasing linguistic competence (Dörnyei and Thurrell, 1991).

Design

With these principles in mind, we have designed *Study Speaking* to create opportunities for learners to experience three different sorts of communicative challenge.

Phase 1: Information tasks

These are problem-solving tasks leading to a concrete pen-and-paper solution. Their completion requires the task partners to resort to the interactional strategies (asking for repetition or clarification, etc.) that will enable them to make sense of target language speech outside the classroom context. The tasks themselves are means rather than ends; they raise the *type* of communicative difficulty that learners will encounter in real life, although the specific details may be more or less contrived. Phase 1 has been influenced by research into classroom language learning both in L1 (Brown and Yule, 1983; Brown, Anderson, Shillcock and Yule, 1984) and also in L2 (Pica and Doughty, 1985; Duff, 1986).

Phase 2: Scenarios

'Scenarios' (Di Pietro, 1987) involve a situation where two people, e.g. student and supervisor, have different personal goals and where each tries to get their own way. The potential for confrontation results in interaction that reflects the unpredictability of such conversation, unlike the scripted 'dialogues' that students may be more familiar with. The scenarios provide experience in activities that require a flexible response under social pressure, of a type that is often missing from the language classroom (Bygate, 1987, 1988).

Phase 3: Seminar skills

Phase 3 brings together the informational strand of Phase 1 and the interpersonal strand of Phase 2. It prepares the learners for participation in seminars, where presentational clarity and persuasiveness form the principal components of effective speaking. Our own research into postgraduate seminars (Lynch and Anderson, 1989) has highlighted specific areas in which foreign students seem to have considerable difficulty, such as focussed questioning and disagreement with the previous speaker. The source of these problems may be cultural or linguistic, or a mixture of the two; either way, learners are likely to gain from the practical experience of organising and performing extended speaking turns of the sort required in formal academic discussion.

Grading

Grading within units

Progress through the three Phases of each unit is graded in terms of *communicative responsibility*, i.e. the degree to which the speaker exercises control over the selection of information. Phase 1 tasks are based on data 'ready to use'; the challenge is to find an appropriate and effective way of putting the information across. In the scenarios in Phase 2, small groups of learners share the responsibility for working out possible conversational moves and countermoves in advance, in the process picking up new language and ideas about communication. Finally, the Phase 3 mini-seminars require the students to gather and organise their own data for a short talk. Here, everyone is individually responsible both for the content and the form of the presentation.

Grading between units

Grading is also built in from unit to unit, in three forms. Firstly, the Phase 1 tasks have been constructed so as to become more complex as the course progresses. Your *Unit notes* include suggestions as to how to adjust the level of complexity to suit the group you are teaching by altering key elements in the materials.

Secondly, there is progression in the type of language that the learner is required to produce. In line with L1 and L2 research into the relative complexity of types of language text (see Anderson and Lynch, 1988 for a review), the Phase 3 tasks move from description in the early units to argument/persuasion in the later ones.

Thirdly, as Phase 3 develops, the speakers give more substantial oral presentations, beginning with brief talks of five minutes or so in Unit 1 and finishing with presentations of 15–20 minutes in *Extension work*.

By varying the demands on the learners in these three ways, the linguistic and cognitive load is gradually increased over the course.

Timing

Each unit should provide material for four lessons of 45 minutes: *Information task* (one lesson), *Scenario* (one lesson) and *Seminar skills* (two lessons), giving an approximate total of 32 lessons or 24 class hours. For groups with less time available, the *Seminar skills* material from the eight units can be used as an autonomous course of 12 hours. *Extension work* is open-ended and can fill the time available after the completion of the *Seminar skills*.

Level

The complete course is best suited to students whose proficiency level is between lower-intermediate and higher-intermediate (approximately IELTS 4.5–6.0, or TOEFL 450–580). This is based on our experience with students in Edinburgh and on that of teachers piloting *Study Speaking* elsewhere.

Learners above IELTS 6.0 or TOEFL 580 might focus on the *Seminar skills* and *Extension work* components. We have allowed for a variety of levels by including in the *Unit notes* suggestions for task-related expressions that could be taught to lower-level students if necessary.

Teacher's guide

Towards the end of the book is a *Teacher's guide* comprising the following: three background sections on general principles, procedures and feedback for each of the three Phases (A *Information tasks*; B *Scenarios*; and C *Seminar skills*); Section D – *Unit notes*; Section E – transcripts and notes on *Sample performances* (see below).

B versions

Materials for most *Information tasks* and all *Scenarios* come in two versions, for A and B partners/groups. The A versions appear in the relevant unit of the students' materials; the B versions are presented in jumbled order between pages 38 and 46. Specific page references are given in Section D – *Unit notes* in the Teacher's guide.

Cassette

Side 1 of the cassette accompanying the book contains the listening materials for the *Seminar skills* work in Units 1–4. Transcripts of the recordings are provided on pages 57–61. If you are teaching this book without the cassette, you will need to use the transcripts in order to give the talks for the comprehension tasks in Units 1–4 yourself.

Side 2 of the cassette contains *Sample performances* by our students of tasks from each Phase. The recordings are transcribed in Section E of the *Teacher's guide*, where we offer comments on points to draw students' attention to in each performance. Bear in mind that these are samples, *not models*; they show what live task performances sound like and their technical quality reflects what they are – recordings from the classroom, not the studio.

We hope you will find the material useful and enjoyable. If you have time to tell us about your experiences of using the book, we would be very glad to hear from you.

Tony Lynch   Institute for Applied Language Studies
Kenneth Anderson   University of Edinburgh
                     21 Hill Place
                     Edinburgh EH8 9DP
                     Scotland – UK

Unit 1   Starting a course

INFORMATION TASK: COURSE STRUCTURE

Partner A

The blank flowchart opposite shows the structure of a Diploma/M.Sc. course in Applied Chaotics. Your partner has information in the form of a 'course glossary', explaining the course components. They will give you the relevant details from their text; your task is to complete the diagram from the information they give you. You may need to ask for repetition or clarification. Remember – Partner B does not have the flowchart.

SCENARIO: BANK

Group A: Student

It is the week before your course starts. A few days ago you opened an account at a bank near the university and were given a piece of paper with the account number. Access to your account is by means of a cashpoint card, which you were told would be sent to your address. It still has not arrived.

The money that you brought with you is nearly finished. You call in at the bank to see if you can take any money out. You have left the account number at home.

The person you speak to is not the one you saw when you opened the account. How will you explain the position to them?

Dip./M.Sc. in Applied Chaotics

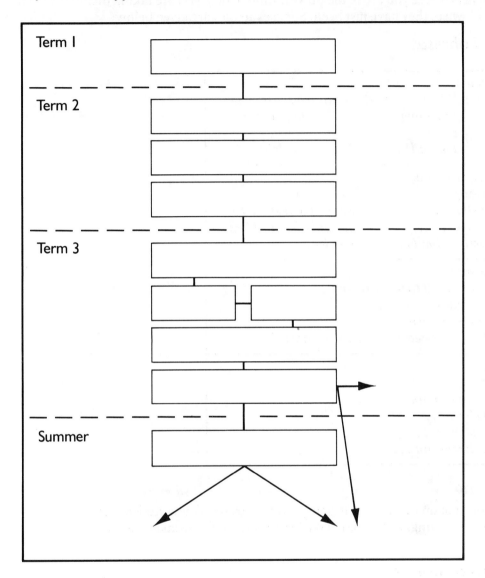

SEMINAR SKILLS: SIGNPOSTING

When giving a seminar presentation it is important to organise the information into a clear and logical order. We have various options for structuring the presentation: in chronological sequence; from most important to least important; from general to particular. Using familiar information structures like these helps to make a presentation 'listener-friendly'.

One way of marking the talk's sections and subsections is to use what are called *signposts*. As the name suggests, these are words and phrases that tell the listeners where you are in the presentation, where you are taking them next and where they have just been. Some examples are given below:

Useful phrases

Introduction		
What I'd like	*to do is (to)*	*discuss . . .*
I'm going		*talk about . . .*
I want		*consider . . .*
I intend		*explain . . .*

Ordering points	
Listing	Time order
Firstly . . .	*First / To begin with*
Secondly (etc.) . . .	*Second / Next / Then*
Lastly / Finally . . .	*Finally . . .*

Transition
I'd like now to move on to . . .
Turning now to . . .
Moving now to . . .
Having looked at (X), let's consider (Y)

Conclusion
So . . .
We've seen that . . .
In short . . .
To sum up . . .
In conclusion . . .

Listening

The short talk on the cassette is one given to a group of new students at a pre-course meeting. Listen and make brief notes on the speaker's main points.

Discussion points

Compare your notes with those of another student. Do you agree on how many sections and subsections there were? Do you have any questions that you would want to ask the speaker? On what basis did she order the information? Could she have made the structure clearer?

Speaking

STAGE 1: PREPARATION

Plan a short talk (three to four minutes) on the topic of student funding in your country. Decide what information you would need to give to listeners who are unfamiliar with the system. This might include such questions as:

who pays for a student's tuition, books, accommodation; how study loans or grants are allocated; whether the arrangements are the same for undergraduate and graduate students; whether your government offers scholarships for study abroad.

STAGE 2: PRACTICE

Give your talk to one other student. They should take notes and ask questions at the end about points that are unclear or need expansion.

Then look at their notes. Have they understood all your main points? Have they recognised your signposts? Think about the questions they asked; could you change the structure or the detail to make the ideas clearer?

Then exchange roles with your partner.

STAGE 3: PRESENTATION

Now work with two other students (not with the same partner as in Stage 2) and take turns in giving your talk a second time. Pay particular attention to the way you signpost a move to a new topic. Check afterwards whether the listeners' notes match what you intended to say. Is any essential information missing from their versions?

STAGE 4: EVALUATION

What did you find when you looked at the other students' notes? Did you discover that:
a) both understood all your main points?
b) they differed in what they had understood?
c) they had misunderstood any parts?

Summary

The content of a presentation is a complex network of ideas and interrelationships; although the details may be clear to *you* as speaker, your listeners need to be guided through the spoken information – and this is where signposts are important.

Unit 2   University systems

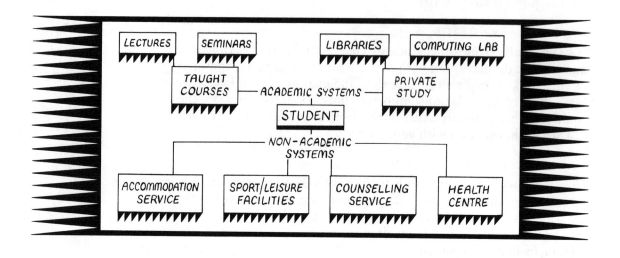

INFORMATION TASK: STUDENT SOCIETIES

In this activity you will be working together with two or three other students, solving a 'jigsaw puzzle' of sentences that make up a paragraph. Your teacher will give each person in your group two different sentences from the paragraph. You have to memorise them. If you want to ask the teacher about the meaning or pronunciation of any of the words, you can.

When you have had time to memorise the sentences, the pieces of paper will be collected in again. **You must not write anything down yet.** Your task is to talk to the others in your group and to establish the correct order of the sentences. When you think you have worked out the original sequence, the teacher will check your solution and tell you what to do next.

Useful phrases

You may find some of these expressions helpful in your group discussion:

> *Mine/Yours must come first/second/next because . . .*
> *That can't be next because . . .*
> *But the word (X) must/could refer to . . .*
> *The next sentence has to be about . . .*
> *What/How about this order: . . .?*

SCENARIO: LIBRARY

Group A: Librarian

You run a small departmental library. It is Monday afternoon of the last week of the summer vacation and you are engaged in your annual stocktaking. Your assistant is away and you are having to carry out the work by yourself. Because of this you have decided to keep the library closed in the morning to allow you to work uninterrupted. So for this week only, the opening hours will be from 2 p.m. to 5 p.m., Monday to Friday.

You have also decided that it is too difficult for you to administer a loan system under these circumstances, so you are not allowing books to be borrowed until the start of the term. The main university library is open as normal: 9 a.m. to 5 p.m. (weekdays).

A foreign student comes in and asks about borrowing books from the library. Plan how best to make the situation clear to them.

SEMINAR SKILLS: DELIVERY

In the previous unit we worked on organising and signalling spoken information, concentrating on *what* you say, as opposed to *how* you say it. But of course the way a person speaks can also influence the audience's understanding. We have called this section 'Delivery', because the word 'pronunciation' tends to be associated with individual sounds. What we want to focus on are two other aspects of spoken English that are known to cause comprehension problems: *stress* and *speed of speaking*.

Stress

Learners of English can become preoccupied with getting the individual sounds right, but may fail to pay attention to the more important problem of word stress. If you produce a word with reasonably correct pronunciation but with incorrectly placed stress, the listener is likely not to understand what you said or to understand something different to what you meant. One example would be the words 'eligible' and 'illegible', where the difference in the sounds of the two words is less important *from the point of view of comprehension* than the correct placement of the word stress:

ELigible   versus   ilLEGible

Discussion point 1: Word stress

The stress pattern in the words below can cause problems for students of English. Say each of them to yourself and underline the syllable that you think carries the main stress.

OCCUR	ACADEMIC	CONCENTRATE
PURPOSE	DEVELOPMENT	PROCESS
TECHNIQUE	EVENT	

Discussion point 2: Sentence stress

Depending which word the speaker places the main stress on, the sentence below could convey different meanings. Can you say which words could carry the main stress, and what the sentence would mean as a result?

A lot of overseas undergraduates have applied for the Diploma.

Speed

Speed is the second major factor in making yourself understood. People learning a foreign language (particularly in the early stages) find that the speakers of that language seem to talk fast. But the same thing can also happen in reverse: native listeners sometimes have difficulty in understanding a foreign speaker's English and say it is because they talk too quickly. Speed is a crucial aspect of successful performance in seminars in a foreign language.

Discussion point 3

One of our students at Edinburgh spoke so rapidly that people had difficulty catching what he said. When a teacher advised him to speak slower in group discussions, he said, 'Why should I slow down? Other people must get used to listening to normal speech.' Do you accept his point of view? Why (not)?

Listening

You are going to hear a short talk in which the speaker explains how people apply for and obtain places on undergraduate courses in Britain. Make notes on the key points in the application process. When you have heard the talk, your teacher will ask you some questions.

Speaking

STAGE 1: PREPARATION

Prepare notes for a brief talk on how students apply for and enter undergraduate courses in your country. Decide on the main stages; make sure you are confident about where to place the *stress* in the key words that you plan to use in the presentation. If you are doubtful about any of them, look up the correct stress in a dictionary or ask the teacher.

STAGE 2: PRACTICE

Give your talk to one other student. Keep in mind the need to *speak slower* at points when you are explaining anything specific to your country that your listener may be unfamiliar with. If they seem to be having difficulty in following you, be prepared to slow down, to repeat or to spell out the words they are having problems with.

The listener should make notes during your talk and ask questions at the end about points that need clarification.

When you have answered their queries, have a look at their notes. Have they understood your main points? Have they noted key terms correctly?

Then exchange roles with your partner.

STAGE 3: PRESENTATION

Now work with two other students (not with the same partner as in Stage 2) and take turns in giving your talk a second time. Pay particular attention to stress and speed as you deal with the key elements in the procedure.

Check afterwards whether the listeners' notes match what you intended to say. Is any essential information missing from their versions?

STAGE 4: EVALUATION

Did you find that the listeners needed to ask for clarification?
Did they ask you to slow down at any point?
Did the tutor make any comments about word stress?
Did you realise that you stressed those words differently?

Summary

Most adults learning a foreign language find it difficult to change their accent. If you want to increase your chances of being understood in English, concentrate on two aspects of the way you deliver the message. Firstly, make sure you are familiar with the word stress of the key terms in your talk. Secondly, reduce your speed of speaking; it may seem unnatural to speak slower than you know you can, but if your listeners cannot understand you, you are failing to communicate – which is the whole point of speaking.

Unit 3   Accommodation

INFORMATION TASK: LAYOUT OF A FLAT

Partner A

Opposite is the outline of a flat. Your partner will tell you how to complete the drawing to show the internal details (rooms, doors, windows). Use a pencil, rather than a pen. You will probably need to ask for repetition and clarification as your partner describes the layout.

Think carefully about what sort of information you would like to hear first. Tell your partner where you want them to begin.

SCENARIO: THE STUDENT ACCOMMODATION OFFICE

Group A: Student

The university term has already started and you still don't have permanent accommodation. You are staying at a guest house, but it is very expensive and you need to find somewhere urgently. Your family is coming to join you in a month's time.

You want: – a two-bedroomed flat with plenty of space;
– a maximum rent of £250 per month;
– somewhere near your department, to save time and money.

There are two ways of finding a flat. One is through the University Accommodation Office. The other is to look for a flat privately, but private flats tend to be more expensive and you need to choose carefully.

The Accommodation Office have already offered you two flats but neither of them has been suitable. You feel that the staff are beginning to lose patience with you. However, you have made another appointment at the Office because you have heard from a student doing your course that there are some unoccupied university flats near your department, and you wonder why the Accommodation Officer has never mentioned them.

How can you (tactfully) ask about these flats?

SEMINAR SKILLS: USING VISUAL AIDS

Visual aids can provide useful support to a spoken presentation; in particular they are an effective means of showing relationships, presenting statistical data or summarising information. However, keep two things in mind: firstly, they are intended to *aid* your oral presentation, not to dominate what you say; secondly, they are *visual*, so they need to be clear, simple and legible.

Discussion point

What are the principal types of visual aid? What are their advantages?

Listening

The speaker on the tape is discussing ways in which students of English can improve the effectiveness of their speaking. His talk involves the flowchart on page 52. Listen to the tape and make notes on what he says.

Speaking

Your talk this time should be related to the theme of accommodation for students in your home country. It could cover any of a number of areas: types, sources and location of accommodation; whether students tend to live at home; whether rents are subsidised; whether particular students are given priority; how you apply for accommodation, etc. You need not cover all of those; be selective in your planning.

STAGE 1: PREPARATION

Decide which points you want to cover. Make a visual aid that will be appropriate to your topic: for example, a *tree diagram* to show the relationship between different categories, a *flowchart* to show the stages in the process of applying for accommodation, a *map* if you want to talk about the location of accommodation in a specific university.

   Remember: The visual aid should not simply duplicate what you are going to say, but should provide support for your presentation.

STAGE 2: PRACTICE

Give your talk to one other student, using the visual aid. See whether any part of your talk seems to be unclear. Do you need to make any adjustments or additions to the aid?

   Then exchange roles with your partner.

STAGE 3: PRESENTATION

Having made any necessary adjustments, give the talk again to two or three new listeners. As before, make sure that the information you give them is as clear as possible. When you have finished, allow them to ask any questions they wish to. Also ask them for their comments on the presentation.

STAGE 4: EVALUATION

Now that you have had the chance to see listeners' reactions to your talk, have you thought of ways of improving the visual aid? Some of the common problems are these:
– it may be *too small* for the audience to see
– the speaker includes *too much detail*
– the information shown may be *inappropriate*

Summary

The main point to remember is that a diagram, map or graph can be a powerful way to explain the relationship between different elements in spoken information. Allow the visual aid to *describe* the information and use your words to *explain and discuss* it.

Timing is critical. If you are using a projector or flipchart, you need to display the visual aid long enough for the audience to read and understand the information. Make a point of checking that everyone has had enough time to take it in (and make notes) before you move on to the next item.

Unit 4   Language

INFORMATION TASK: LANGUAGE LEARNING

This task is based on another 'jigsaw' paragraph like the one in Unit 2 – with one important difference. You will again be given jumbled sentences to memorise and re-order, but this time one of the sentences from the paragraph is missing. When your group has reached a solution to the problem, you will also have to decide what the content of the missing sentence might be.

SCENARIO: LANGUAGE COURSES

Group A: Course director

You are in charge of English courses provided by a university to help overseas students. The students have to take a language test (listening, reading and writing) at the start of the academic year. If necessary, they then take any of three evening courses in the first term (also in listening, reading and writing).

There are always more students than places, so you have to restrict the numbers and you give priority to the weaker students. Many of the people who apply to do the courses do not really need further tuition; as a general rule, you do not accept anyone onto the courses who has scored more than 60% on the relevant section of the test. Exceptions are made, because no test is perfect. If you have evidence (such as a report from a supervisor) that someone is really having problems, you sometimes accept them with a score of over 60%.

A student has made an appointment to see you. They have applied for all three courses, but have not been accepted; their test scores were Listening 70%, Reading 65% and Writing 62%. They probably want you to change your mind. This year there has been greater demand for courses than ever before. How will you find out whether they have a genuine language problem? What advice will you give them?

SEMINAR SKILLS: GETTING CLARIFICATION

When using a foreign language, we have to get used to dealing with situations where we do not understand, or only partly understand, what the speaker has said. In a seminar, where time may be short, it is important to make it clear to the speaker precisely what your problem is. If you ask a very general question you may find that the speaker simply produces a repetition of what they said before.

Useful phrases

Non-comprehension
I'm sorry, I didn't understand what you said about (X).
                  catch
          could you repeat
What does (X) mean?

Partial comprehension
What did you mean when you said (X)?
Could you be more specific about (X)?
          expand a little on   what you said about (X)?
          give an example of
          explain in more detail

Getting confirmation *So you're telling me that I can't . . .?* *So what you're saying is that . . .?* *So you mean that . . .?*

Listening

Your teacher is going to play you a short talk about the differences between two languages: English and Outlandic. Listen carefully and make notes. At the end of the talk, ask the teacher for clarification of any points you have not fully understood.

Speaking

STAGE I: PREPARATION

Think about the general differences in grammatical structure between your own language and English. Note down the main points of difference, but do not write complete sentences. Among the things you could consider are: tenses, articles, word order, pronouns and question forms.

STAGE 2: PRACTICE

Using your notes, describe the differences to a partner. Limit your talk to around five minutes. Allow them to ask you for any additional clarification that they feel they need. Be prepared to expand or exemplify what you have said.

Then exchange roles of speaker and listener.

STAGE 3: PRESENTATION

Form a new trio with two other students. Take turns at giving your talk as the others take notes. Answer the questions that your listeners may need to ask you. Think in particular about ways of making clearer the points that your Stage 2 partner asked you to clarify.

STAGE 4: EVALUATION

Were you able to make the differences clearer the second time? Are there still points that you would like the teacher to help you to put into English?

Summary

As a listener in a seminar you should not feel embarrassed about asking the speaker to repeat or clarify ideas that you were unable to follow first time round. But time (and patience) can quickly be used up if you do not make clear what it is that needs clarification.

Unit 5   Teaching

INFORMATION TASK: DEPARTMENTAL ORGANISATION

Partner A

Your partner has an incomplete diagram showing the way teaching is organised in a university department. From the text below select the information that you think will help them to complete the diagram.

Departmental teaching is organised into three main areas: courses for undergraduates, courses for postgraduates, and supervision for research students. In the case of undergraduate teaching, the day-to-day running of courses is in the hands of a Director of Studies, who works with a number of tutors. Postgraduate taught courses such as Master's courses are the responsibility of a Course Director, assisted by staff in the role of tutors (teaching small groups) or supervisors (when advising students individually on course assignments). Postgraduate students doing a research degree work with a supervisor (or sometimes two), whose job it is to provide overall guidance rather than detailed instruction.

There are no strict divisions between academic staff in these three areas. The same person might, for example, both teach on undergraduate and postgraduate courses, and also supervise research students. The person with ultimate responsibility for all teaching areas is the Head of Department, and it is to them that you can go for help if you are dissatisfied with any of the teaching you receive.

SCENARIO: POSTPONING AN ESSAY

Group A: Student

You are working on an essay which has to be handed in by tomorrow, Friday. Although you are normally well-organised and have worked hard on this particular essay, you now realise that you will not get it finished on time.

   Your main problem has been that you needed to use data on your home country, which is available only in one book. When you looked for it in the library, it was out on loan. You asked for the book to be recalled, but it came back only yesterday. You need time to analyse and report on the data, and you think it will take you at least another two days to complete the essay.

   Unfortunately, your tutor is well-known for being very strict about deadlines. Also, you had to ask for an extension once before when you were ill, and you are embarrassed to ask again. How can you best ask for the deadline to be extended until Monday?

SEMINAR SKILLS: QUESTIONING

Speakers are expected to allow time at the end of their presentation for questions and discussion. Many people would say that this question-and-answer stage is at least as important as the initial presentation. However, questioning can be a problematic aspect of seminar performance. Often the speaker misunderstands a question (and not only when the questioner is a non-native speaker), because the point is lost in an over-long sentence.

   A practical solution is to keep your question short. Don't forget that the presenter may not be sure, when you start to speak, that you are asking a question – you might be wanting to disagree. So you need to make clear:

		Example:
a) that it's a question		*'I have a question . . .*
b) what the topic is		*. . . about assessment on the course.*
c) what the point is		*What is the overall balance between*
		the examinations and the project work?'

Discussion point 1

It is sometimes suggested that the speaker should repeat or summarise each question asked from the audience, before beginning to give an answer. Why is this advice given?

Discussion point 2

Questions and answers are not always straightforward. *The speaker* who is asked a question by a listener may understand the question but be unable (or unwilling) to give an answer, in which case, they may *avoid* giving a direct answer. Below are some examples. Can you think of others?

> Avoiding an answer
> *(X) is important but it's too complex for us to deal with here.*
> *I think we have to focus on (Y) rather than (X).*
> *It's too early for us to say whether . . .*
> *We don't have enough evidence to show that . . .*
> *That's not something I've had time to deal with, but . . .*

Discussion point 3

The listener may want to say that the answer they have received is inadequate:

> Following up a question
> *That's not really what I was asking. My question was about . . .*
> *Perhaps I didn't make my question clear. In fact what I asked was . . .*
> *I think you've answered a slightly different question.*
> *I've understood that but what I actually had in mind was . . .*

These expressions are relatively polite and formal. What words could you omit from each example to make them more direct? What type of words are they?

Speaking

STAGE 1: PREPARATION

The basis for the practice in questioning will be a five to ten minute talk on the organisation and methods of a university course that you have attended. You could select from: the type of teaching (lecture, seminar, tutorial); the way the course was structured (compulsory subjects, options, individual research); access to the teaching staff; the problems you encountered (which might range from the teaching style of specific lecturers to the scarcity of suitable library materials); and so on.

For the purpose of this talk, leave out any problems to do with the *content* of the course; concentrate on the structure and methods.

STAGE 2: PRESENTATION

Working with two partners, take turns in giving your talk and taking notes. As before, the listeners should ask questions at the end, but this time pay particular attention to the way that you ask the questions (*listener*) and answer them (*speaker*). You can refer back to the expressions given under the Discussion points.

STAGE 3: EVALUATION

Listener   Did you understand the answers?
Were they appropriate to the question you had asked?
Were you satisfied with the answers?

Speaker   Did you understand the point of the questions?
Did you have answers? *If so*, were you able to present them
clearly?
If not, did you admit you didn't know, or did you manage to
avoid an answer?

SUMMARY

The question-and-answer stage is important but can be frustrating if the
questioner does not make clear the scope or point of their question. Speakers
can help themselves (and the audience) by summarising questions in order to
confirm or highlight the topic for the next part of the discussion.

Unit 6   Health

INFORMATION TASK: MEDICAL TREATMENT

The task is similar to the one in Unit 4: you have to work out the correct
order for a jigsaw paragraph. Again, one sentence will be missing from the
set you are given by your teacher and you have to identify where it should
come in the paragraph and what it would say. It's a bit trickier than last
time!

SCENARIO: DOCTOR'S SURGERY

Group A: Doctor

You work at the Student Health Centre. It is getting close to the university
exam time, when students may develop temporary symptoms, due to stress,
working late and drinking excessive amounts of coffee. In addition, foreign
students are perhaps more prone to stress caused by sociocultural problems.
Very occasionally, you get someone who hopes to avoid exams by claiming
to be ill.

   It is Friday afternoon. A student has made a second appointment to see
you. They first presented on Wednesday complaining of stomach pains, but
you found nothing abnormal, and you are confident that it is a mild stomach
upset. You prescribed a mild antacid mixture to calm the stomach and
suggested they should try to relax. You asked them to come back in a week's
time.

   This particular student had expected to be referred to a consultant straight
away but you reassured them that there was nothing seriously wrong.

   Your general feeling about this patient is that they are simply overanxious.
How can you reassure them that there is nothing to worry about and that
they should continue the treatment you prescribed?

SEMINAR SKILLS: NON-VERBAL SIGNALS

Although this is an English language course, it is important to remember that our spoken messages may be supplemented (or even changed) by the *unspoken*, non-verbal elements of face-to-face communication – what is often called 'body language'. Body language is of special importance in communication between people from different countries, since their cultural expectations and experience will tend to make them interpret these non-verbal signals in different ways.

Discussion point 1

First, a question about body language in general. In your country, would it be considered: (a) offensive, (b) complimentary, or (c) meaningless to do the following as a comment on what someone has just said:
– to tap or touch the side of your head with your index finger?
– to make a circle shape with a thumb and one finger?

Discussion point 2

Now the more specific area of seminar presentation. What would be your impression of a speaker who:
a) did not look up from their notes?
b) shifted their weight from foot to foot as they spoke?
c) kept scratching their head?
d) chose to sit on the table (rather than standing up or sitting on a chair)?

Discussion point 3

Which non-verbal signals would indicate to you that a speaker is:
a) confident?
b) poorly prepared?
c) shy?

Eye contact

Many non-verbal signals are unconscious and difficult to control, but there is one important aspect of non-verbal behaviour in seminars that is relatively open to control: *eye contact*. In one-to-one conversation a person who keeps looking away from the other and avoiding eye contact with them might give the impression of being, for example, respectful, deceitful or shy – depending on the local culture. The situation is obviously different when there is *one* speaker and *many* listeners, as in a seminar. Speakers cannot look at everyone in the audience all the time and so they seem to adopt one of various alternatives:
a) look at one person all the time;
b) look at some people most of the time;
c) look at nobody, e.g. by looking over the audience's heads at the wall or looking down at their notes;
d) look at all of the listeners some of the time.

Discussion point 4

From the social/communicative point of view, which do you think is the best strategy? Why?

Discussion point 5

This question of eye contact may appear rather trivial, but consider the following example. A Sudanese postgraduate on one of our courses at Edinburgh was giving a seminar and the teacher noticed that the only person that he looked at during his presentation was another student from Sudan. The teacher happened to be sitting on the other side of the classroom and was struck by the fact that the speaker had not looked towards his side of the room.

After the presentation, the teacher asked the listeners to give the presentation a score out of ten. The scores from the students who had been sitting next to the Sudanese listener were consistently higher than those from members of the audience on the teacher's side of the room.

What do you think caused the difference in reaction?

Speaking

The topic for your talk this time is medicine in your home country. Again, you have a wide range of possible issues to talk about: types of treatment (conventional or complementary medicine); the procedures for getting treated; the way medical treatment is funded; popular remedies for minor ailments, e.g. headaches and nosebleeds; private and public health services; the status of doctors and other medical personnel; etc.

Try to distribute eye contact equally among your listeners as you give the presentation. If you decide to use some form of visual aid, e.g. the blackboard, don't forget to talk to the audience, rather than looking only at the visual.

STAGE 1: PREPARATION

You have only five to ten minutes, so you will need to limit the scope of what you want to say. Remember that some of the things you may want to discuss will be unfamiliar to your listeners. Make sure that your notes are clear and well-ordered.

STAGE 2: PRESENTATION

Work in a trio, taking it in turns to give your talk. The two listeners should take notes as usual and ask questions at the end to get points confirmed or clarified, or to discuss points they disagree with.

STAGE 3: EVALUATION

Think about the questions your listeners needed to ask you. Were they about points that you had already mentioned or were they things you had not thought of including? If you had mentioned them, why were the questions necessary?

Did you have to *repeat* or *expand* what you had said? If you had to repeat information, could that have been prevented by attention to any of the areas we have covered so far:
– signposting
– delivery (stress and speed)
– visual aids
Did you make a conscious effort to maintain eye contact?

Summary

We do not communicate only with our mouths. In face-to-face conversation, non-verbal signals are an essential unconscious part of our message; in seminars, careful distribution of eye contact can help to make your audience feel involved and to maintain their attention and interest.

Unit 7 Evaluation

INFORMATION TASK: TRAVEL GRANT COMMITTEE

You are a member of a committee at a university department which is
responsible for deciding on applications for travel grants. Four students in
the department have applied for money to attend an international congress
in Toronto later this year. The department has a small Overseas Students'
Fund, which would be sufficient to cover the expenses (air fare, conference
fee and accommodation) for one person.

Each committee member will be given information about one of the four
applicants, in the form of a brief reference written by their tutor or
supervisor. (The teacher will tell you where to find the information.)

Read the reference carefully and select the relevant facts. Summarise them
so that the other committee members can take notes. When you all have
sufficient information on the four students, the next step is to decide which
of the applicants should be awarded the travel grant.

In order to reach your decision, you will need to discuss such things as the
likely benefit to the department if a particular student were to attend the
Toronto congress.

SCENARIO: EXAMINATION RESULTS

Group A: Student

You are about to start the second term of an M.Sc. course. There was a 'mock' exam at the end of last term and you don't think you have done very well. You had in fact expected not to do very well, because most of the first term subjects were new to you. The topics for the second term are more familiar and you expect to do better on them.

You feel determined to work harder this term. This may mean you may have to concentrate on your studies, avoiding 'distractions' such as the sports and social activities that took up some of your time in Term 1.

Your supervisor has asked to see you to discuss the exam scores. If your result wasn't very good, what reasons can you suggest?

SEMINAR SKILLS: CONCLUDING

The transition from the presentation to the follow-up discussion is an important point in the seminar, for two reasons:

1. it provides an opportunity for the main speaker to *summarise* what they have said, reminding listeners of the main points covered in the talk;
2. it acts as an *invitation* to the audience to respond to the content of the talk.

It is very easy in the heat of the moment – particularly if you have overrun the time allowed for your talk – to forget the conclusion. No matter how good your presentation has been, it will be improved by your giving the listeners a clear, concise summary of what you have said.

Discussion point 1

What do you think is the best way of presenting a summary of your main points?

Discussion point 2

Below are a number of expressions inviting the audience to contribute. Read through them and decide whether each of them would make a strong or a weak ending to your presentation.

Concluding
    a) *That's all I have time for. Any questions?*
    b) *I think I'll stop there to leave time for questions.*
    c) *That covers the main points. If you have comments or questions, I'll be happy to hear them.*
    d) *Time is getting short so I'd better take questions now.*

Speaking

The majority of university courses involve written examinations at some point. Some people believe that written exams are an inefficient way of evaluating a student's performance on a course. What is your view? Prepare a talk presenting your opinion of written exams. You should aim to *persuade* the listeners to accept your point of view, rather than simply describing your own experience. You may want to mention both positive and negative aspects of exams, but you should make clear in the conclusion what your position is.

STAGE 1: PREPARATION

Plan and make notes for a five to ten minute talk. Pay particular attention to the way you plan the conclusion:
1. the way you introduce your summary;
2. the form in which you remind the audience of the main points;
3. your invitation to the listeners to participate in the discussion.

STAGE 2: PRESENTATION

Work with two other students, taking turns as speaker and listeners/note-takers. Each of you should give your presentation and answer factual questions. Keep the discussion of each other's points until after the third speaker's presentation, so that all of you have a chance to argue your case before the general discussion.

After the general discussion, you should complete Stage 3.

STAGE 3: EVALUATION

Compare the notes you used in the talk with the ones the listeners took as you spoke. Were they able to follow the main points in your presentation? Were you able to answer their questions satisfactorily? Which parts of your argument did they accept? How could you strengthen your presentation? Did you include the three elements of the conclusion – signalling the summary, giving the summary and asking for listeners' questions?

Summary

It is sensible to round off your presentation by providing your listeners with a summary that reminds them of the main points. Bear in mind the conventional wisdom about talks: *'Tell them what you are going to say. Say it. Tell them what you have said.'*

Unit 8   Research

INFORMATION TASK: RESEARCH TRENDS

The table below shows data on postgraduate research grants in Britain for 1977 and 1987. The details missing from your version of the table are available in your partner's table. Without looking at each other's data, agree on answers to the following questions:

1. What are the main areas of difference between the figures for the two years?
2. Decide which form of diagram would offer the best way of highlighting those differences.
3. Draw the diagram.
4. Discuss the possible reasons for the changes between 1977 and 1987.

Government research grants to postgraduates at UK universities in 1977 and 1987				
	1977	%	1987	%
Biological sciences	1 832	15.9	1 974	16.4
Chemistry	1 444		1 599	13.2
Information science	51		2 639	21.9
Mathematics	692	6.0		5.6
Physics	1 050	9.2	584	4.8
	3 285	28.5	1 402	11.6
Others		27.5	3 201	26.5
Total	11 529	100.0	12 072	100.0
Total expenditure	£30 m			

(Based on the Central Statistical Office Annual Abstract of Statistics 1989, London: HMSO)

SCENARIO: RESEARCH PROPOSAL

Group A: Head of Department

The university where you work operates a 'probationary year' system. This means that anyone who hopes to register for a Ph.D. is required to spend one year as a 'supervised postgraduate student', doing the preliminary work leading up to a research proposal. The proposal has to be presented to a committee of three members of the departmental staff by the end of the academic year.

One overseas student in your Department has complained to you of unfair treatment, since their research committee has rejected their proposal. Instead, they felt that the work so far suggested the student might be capable of achieving M.Litt. standard but not Ph.D. level. The committee's principal objections were to (a) the lack of an adequate theoretical basis to the work, and (b) the student's lack of proficiency in English.

You have talked the matter over with your colleagues and it has been agreed that the student should be registered for an M.Litt. for the moment, but should submit a revised proposal within six months. Provided the revised proposal is strong enough, then they may be registered for a Ph.D. at that point.

You have asked the student to come to see you. You are interested to hear their side of the story. Think about what questions you want to ask; also, plan how to tell the student about the suggestion you have agreed with the members of the research committee.

SEMINAR SKILLS: DISAGREEING

As a *seminar speaker* you should expect your presentation to lead to questions and discussion from members of the audience. You need to be ready to respond to contributions from listeners who wish to disagree with or challenge what you have said, either on points of detail or in general. People from different cultures deal with disagreement in very different ways; some show that they disagree with you by saying *nothing at all* (silence = lack of acceptance) or by saying *a great deal* (continual questions, objections, negative comments).

Discussion point 1

Imagine two seminars in a university department in your country, on the same topic and for the same audience of postgraduate students. One is given by a lecturer; the other is given by one of the department's students. Would you expect the listeners to express disagreement in different ways in the two seminars? Why (or why not) and in what way?

Discussion point 2

The table below shows data from our research into postgraduate seminars at the University of Edinburgh:

Distribution of contributions to seminars by native (N) and non-native (NN) students		
	N	NN
Statement of opinion	27%	21%
Disagreement	24%	11%
Questions	37%	55%
Clarification requests	11%	9%

(From Lynch and Anderson, 1989)

As you see, we found that overseas students asked more questions (55% of their contributions, compared to 37% for British students) but disagreed less often (11% compared to 24%).

  Can you suggest why the overseas students' pattern of contribution in seminars was different to that of the British students?

Discussion point 3

One of the features of British seminars is that people tend to disagree without actually using the word '*disagree*', and simply use the word 'but' to indicate that they are objecting to what has been said. Below are some examples. Can you think of other ways of showing you disagree without using that verb?

Disagreeing
  But don't you think that . . .?
  I see what you mean but . . .
  But isn't it really a question of . . .?
  But what about . . .?
  But surely . . .?

Speaking

In this final unit we leave the choice of topic for the presentation up to you. Select a controversial subject that is likely to lead to a lively exchange of views at the end of the talk. One option would be to think of an issue related to the overall theme for this unit: research. In most academic fields there is disagreement about the focus, methods or conclusions of recent studies.

STAGE I: PREPARATION

Make notes for a presentation of about ten minutes. As well as planning the structure and content of your talk, think about the points on which your listeners are likely to disagree with you. Prepare ways of dealing with those objections.

STAGE 2 : PRESENTATION

Speaker   Work with two other students. Take it in turns to give your talk. Allow up to ten minutes for the presentation and five minutes to deal with the others' questions and comments.

Listeners Make careful notes as you listen. At the end, use the opportunity to question and disagree. Try to make sure that your questions and criticisms are clear to the speaker.

STAGE 3 : EVALUATION

When you have all given your talks, reflect on how your own talk went:
   How could you have improved the presentation?
   Did the listeners accept your arguments?
   Were you able to answer the points they made after the talk?

Then think about the other students' talks:
   Were there points that you didn't understand the first time?
   If so, were you able to clear them up through questions?

   Did you disagree with anything the speaker said?
   If so, did you express your objections?

   Did you feel you were able to express *precisely* what your objections were?
   If not, ask the teacher to suggest a way of putting it into English.

Evaluation form

On pages 53–4 you will find a *Seminar evaluation form*. Read through the points listed there and discuss any doubts or questions with your teacher. Use it to assess *your own* presentation in this unit.

Summary

Disagreement, challenge and argument are important elements of academic communication in any culture. Exactly *how* people on your course express disagreement will vary. Even in different departments of the same institution there can be different expectations about how to disagree acceptably.

At one seminar we heard a lecturer complain to an overseas student who had asked a question and accepted an inadequate answer from the presenter, 'You're being too polite. Don't be polite – be critical!' You will need to observe whether local expectations match those of that particular lecturer.

B versions

INFORMATION TASK 7: TRAVEL GRANT COMMITTEE

Reference 4

Despina Patsourakis is doing the second year of an undergraduate course. At 29, she is older than most of the other students on the course. Her first degree (taken in Greece) was in Law. After working for four years in a commercial law practice in Athens, she decided to change career and to return to university. She would have to be described as a solid and steady worker, but by no means brilliant. However, her proposal for a presentation at the Toronto conference has already been accepted. She speaks English confidently but rather too quickly.

SCENARIO 5: POSTPONING AN ESSAY

Group B: Tutor

The students on one of the postgraduate courses that you teach on are due to hand in their third course essay tomorrow (Friday). One of your tutorial students has asked to see you and it is probably to ask for an extension of the essay deadline. Your general rule is that if an essay comes in late, you don't mark it. If there seems to be a genuine reason, then you make an exception. This particular student has already had an extension for an earlier essay, for health reasons.

   You have a very tight work schedule and planned to mark all the students' essays over the weekend, because next Wednesday you are chairing a one-day conference and will have no time for marking. This makes it very hard for you to accept a late essay.

   How will you react if the student does want an extension?

INFORMATION TASK 1: COURSE STRUCTURE

Partner B

The information below is a 'course glossary' explaining various components of a 12-month postgraduate course. Your partner has a flowchart which corresponds to the information given in your text, but the boxes in their diagram are blank. Your task is to give them the details from the glossary that will help them to complete their diagram. Remember – you will need to give the information clearly as your partner has no text to help them.

Diploma/M.Sc. in Applied Chaotics: Assessment

Dissertation
Students who pass the taught part of the course (the first nine months) are allowed to proceed to the dissertation. This is an extended piece of work on a topic of your choice and occupies the three summer months. It is important to note that the M.Sc. degree is *not awarded automatically* to students who have completed and handed in their dissertation. If you fail to reach the required standard in the dissertation, you are awarded the Diploma.

Examinations
Examinations are held in Term 3 and comprise two separate written papers of three hours each. Exam A contains questions on the core subjects of the course; Exam B deals with option subjects. A 'mock' exam is held at the end of the first term. The results do not count towards your overall assessment, but provide some indication of how well you are coping with the course as a whole and which areas require particular attention.

External Examiner
All departments in the University are required to appoint an External Examiner for their degree courses. The Examiner is normally a widely-respected academic from another university, who is expected to act as an impartial observer, ensuring quality and consistency of assessment. All marks (for practicals, projects or examinations) have to be regarded as provisional until after the Examiners' Meeting, which takes place at the end of the third term. One of the principal functions of the meeting is to decide whether students should (a) fail the course, (b) be awarded a Pass at Diploma level, or (c) proceed to the dissertation.

Practicals
You have to complete two short practical assignments (2–3,000 words) during the second term. Practical 1 involves the reporting of

a small-scale experiment, to a specification with which you will be provided; Practical 2 requires you to carry out a statistical analysis of survey data.

Projects

These are longer papers (4–5,000 words) based on individual research, on a topic which you decide in consultation with a supervisor. Project 1 is handed in halfway through the second term, and Projects 2 and 3 in the third. Project 3 takes the form of a proposal for the summer dissertation.

SCENARIO 6: DOCTOR'S SURGERY

Group B: Student

You have had pains in your stomach for several days and you feel generally unwell. Two days ago you went to see a doctor at the Student Health Centre, who examined you and prescribed some tablets. The medicine seems to have had no effect; in fact, you feel worse and can't sleep properly. You are already anxious about your exams, which start in a couple of weeks; now the worry about your health is making it difficult to concentrate on your revision.

You think that the problem is more serious and that perhaps you didn't explain it clearly enough. The doctor gave you a brief examination and just told you to take the medicine and 'try to relax' for a week or so.

It is now Friday afternoon and the Health Centre closes at the weekend. Monday is a public holiday. You don't want to have to wait until Tuesday before getting attention. How can you persuade the doctor to let you see a specialist, or to change the diagnosis? How can you describe the pain that you have been having?

INFORMATION TASK 7: TRAVEL GRANT COMMITTEE

Reference 2

Lalitha Shastri is in the second year of Ph.D. research. She is shy and quiet, but immensely hard-working. She is now 29 and has held the post of Assistant Lecturer at the University of Madras for four years; she is expected to return to that post on the completion of her studies. Despite problems of ill health, she is making good progress in her doctoral work and proposes to give a paper at the Toronto conference based on her research so far. Her English is competent but strongly accented.

SCENARIO 4: LANGUAGE COURSES

Group B: Student

You are worried about your English; most of the other students on your academic course are native speakers, and you feel at a disadvantage. Before the start of the term you took a language test with other overseas students and scored 70% on listening, 65% on reading and 62% on writing. This seems to you a rather poor set of scores, as you have been used to scoring 80% or more in your home country.

The university runs first term evening courses in listening, reading and writing. You have applied to take all three, but you have had a letter from the course director saying the courses were only open to people with lower scores than you.

You have made an appointment to speak to the course director, to see if you can be allowed onto the courses. What reasons can you give for needing to take further tuition?

INFORMATION TASK 5: DEPARTMENTAL ORGANISATION

Partner B

Your partner has a text containing the information you need to complete the diagram. They do not know what your diagram looks like. Get them to give you the information you require. Ask them to repeat and clarify as necessary.

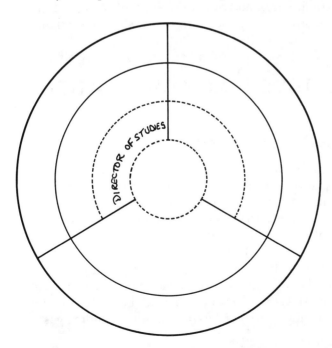

SCENARIO 2: LIBRARY

Group B: Student

Your academic course begins next week. You have been given a preliminary reading list of books that you are expected to read before term starts. Although some are available in the shops, they are very expensive. According to notes on the reading list, all of them are in the departmental library.

The problem is that the departmental library's opening hours are restricted to afternoons and one of the other students has told you that the librarian has decided not to operate a lending service this week.

You decide to see if the librarian will allow you to borrow books. Can you think of good reasons that might persuade them?

INFORMATION TASK 7: TRAVEL GRANT COMMITTEE

Reference 3

Ahmed Al-Buanain from Qatar is 47 years old. He is married and his family are with him. After some years as a senior lecturer at his home university, he is now in his first postgraduate year. He hopes to do a Ph.D. but, as he has not yet submitted his full research proposal to his study committee, he has not yet been promoted to the status of a Ph.D. student. His progress has been rather slow; he is determined and thorough, but says he has been worried about his children's problems with health and school. He has attended many national and international conferences, and intends to send in a proposal for Toronto, although he has not done so yet. His written English is better than his spoken English.

SCENARIO 3: THE STUDENT ACCOMMODATION OFFICE

Group B: Accommodation officer

It is the first week of term and you are extremely busy. An overseas student has made an appointment with you. In general, you try to give overseas students special priority, as they are normally unable to arrange accommodation in advance. But this particular student seems to be rather difficult to please; you have already offered them two flats, but they wouldn't take either of them.

There is in fact a block of two-bedroomed student flats very near this student's department, but it is being renovated at the moment. The work will not be finished for another five or six weeks, so you haven't been able to offer them. When the flats are ready, they will be £270 per month, excluding gas and electricity charges.

You intend to offer the student a large two-bedroomed flat about 15 minutes by bus from their department. The rent is £285, including heating. You have decided that if the student is not happy with what you offer them today, you will suggest that they look for private accommodation. How can you give them that advice without appearing unhelpful?

SCENARIO 8: RESEARCH PROPOSAL

Group B: Student

The university where you are a research student operates a 'probationary year' system; anyone who hopes to do a Ph.D. has to spend one year as a 'supervised postgraduate student', doing preliminary work leading to a research proposal. The proposal is presented to a committee of three members of the departmental staff at the end of the academic year.

Your committee met recently and interviewed you, but things did not go well. All three members of the committee (your supervisor and two other lecturers) were very critical of your proposal. They decided that it was not strong enough to be accepted; instead, they were prepared to accept you for an M.Litt. You have asked to see the Head of the Department, as you feel you have been treated unfairly.

You have had a number of problems. Firstly, the topic you are working on is not one you chose yourself; it was stipulated by the institution where you work in your home country. As you receive a government grant, you could not object to the topic. Secondly, your scholarship is for three years and is specific to Ph.D. research. If for any reason you do not obtain a Ph.D., you will be expected to pay the scholarship back. Thirdly, you were not able to bring your family with you; the separation from them has made you feel very depressed. Lastly, you feel that you have had very little contact with your Department – either with other research students or with the staff. You had expected to see your supervisor often, but have had only half a dozen meetings in the year.

The Head of Department has agreed to see you for 'a brief word'. You are not sure whether the decision can be changed. Think of the possible ways the conversation might develop and plan what you will say.

INFORMATION TASK 3: LAYOUT OF A FLAT

Partner B

You have to describe the layout of the flat overleaf, so that your partner can fill in the details on their plan, which shows only the L shape of the outside walls and the front door.

Before starting to describe the flat, it is important to plan how to give the information: where to start, what sort of information to give, how to check that the listener has understood.

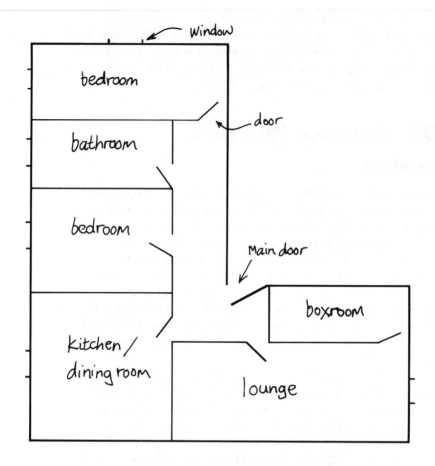

INFORMATION TASK 7: TRAVEL GRANT COMMITTEE

Reference 1

Michael Lo is 21 years old and is currently in the third year of an undergraduate course. Although he has no previous experience of academic conferences, he is a gifted student of great promise; his performances in the final examinations for the first two years have been outstanding, and he achieved the highest marks in both examinations. He is a native of Hong Kong and speaks fluent English.

SCENARIO 7: EXAMINATION RESULTS

Group B: Supervisor

It is the first week of the second term of an M.Sc. course. The students took a 'mock' exam at the end of Term 1 and you have arranged to see each of the students you are supervising, to let them know their results.

One overseas student is causing you and the other lecturers particular concern. Some of the questions they ask during lectures suggest that they have misunderstood quite basic points. It is not clear whether this is due to poor English or to a lack of background knowledge. They contribute very little to tutorial discussions. Their only piece of writing so far (apart from the exam paper) was disorganised and very hard to follow.

In the 'mock' exam, most of their answers were off the point and their overall result was a definite fail. You and your colleagues have discussed the case at a Departmental meeting and the general view is that this student is at risk of failing the M.Sc. In the light of their apparent language problems, it was decided that they should be required to attend an English evening course this term.

As the student appears to have difficulty understanding spoken English, you will need to think carefully about how to make clear to them the potential seriousness of the situation.

INFORMATION TASK 8: RESEARCH TRENDS

The table below shows data on postgraduate research grants in Britain for 1977 and 1987. The details missing from your version of the table are available in your partner's table. Without looking at each other's data, agree on answers to the following questions:

1. What are the main areas of difference between the figures for the two years?
2. Decide which form of diagram would offer the best way of highlighting those differences.
3. Draw the diagram.
4. Discuss the possible reasons for the changes between 1977 and 1987.

Government research grants to postgraduates at UK universities in 1977 and 1987				
	1977		1987	
		%		%
	1 832	15.9	1 974	16.4
Chemistry	1 444	12.5	1 599	13.2
		0.4	2 639	21.9
Mathematics	692		673	5.6
Physics		9.2	584	4.8
Social sciences	3 285	28.5	1 402	
Others	3 175	27.5	3 201	26.5
Total	11 529	100.0	12 072	100.0
Total expenditure			£71 m	

(Based on the Central Statistical Office Annual Abstract of Statistics 1989, London: HMSO)

SCENARIO 1: BANK

Group B: Bank teller/clerk

A foreign student comes into your branch, saying that they opened an account some days ago. They have not received their cashpoint card and want to make a cash withdrawal.

You ask for the person's name. Your records show that an account has been opened in a similar name but the spelling is slightly different. This makes you suspicious.

You cannot authorise a withdrawal without proper identification. The customer would have been given an account number when they opened the account, so you should ask for this. As the senior staff are out at lunch, you have to decide yourself whether or not to let the customer have any money.

How can you check the student's identity without appearing to distrust them?

Extension work

Having completed the eight units, there may be time in your course for you to go on to a further stage of seminar skills practice. We have called it *Extension work*, since it marks a development from what you have been doing so far, in three ways: (1) it allows you to work on more specialised topics; (2) it gives you practice in delivering longer presentations; (3) the seminars are held as whole-class activities, rather than in the small-group format used in the eight units. *Extension work* is designed to act as a bridge between the structured tasks in *Study Speaking* and the demands of real-life seminars.

Each seminar consists of three parts (preceded by a planning stage), as shown below:

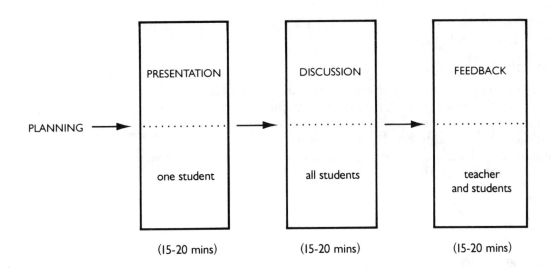

PROCEDURE

Planning

Decide on a topic for your seminar. If the class includes people from a range of subject areas, then you will need to plan the structure and content of your presentation in such a way as to make it accessible to those who may not share your specialist background knowledge.

Remember that the idea is to present a *seminar*, not a *lecture*. In other words, you should select a topic on which you think the other students will be able to ask questions and contribute to discussion.

In the seminar itself you should practise your ability to *speak* English, not your skill in *reading aloud*. So don't write a complete script for your talk; prepare short notes.

Bear in mind that you have no more than 15–20 minutes for your talk. Don't prepare too many notes; try not to cover too much ground.

It is a good idea to rehearse your presentation at home so that you get thoroughly familiar with the material and also see how long it takes to deliver the talk. We find that in general a presentation takes about 25–50% more time when you do it for real than when you rehearse it. If you can, record yourself giving the talk so that you can listen to the tape to see which sections of the talk need improvement.

Presentation

During the presentation, the listeners will be taking notes. They may not interrupt with questions but are encouraged to raise points at the end of the talk.

If you use the board or projector to make content and structure clearer to the audience, there are two points to remember: (1) look at the listeners and not the visual aid; (2) allow the audience plenty of time to take in the information.

Keep an eye on the clock – the teacher will ask you to wind up if you have not finished by the end of the allotted time.

Discussion

Some listeners will want to ask you questions in this second segment of the seminar, or to discuss what you have said. Be patient when they ask you for explanation and clarification; if they have questions to ask or points to make, it shows they are interested in what you have told them.

Summarise/check each question to make sure you (and the other listeners) have understood it correctly.

Feedback

As speaker, you will get two forms of comment on your seminar performance:

1. At the end of the discussion segment, *the other students* fill in an *Evaluation form* (as used in Unit 8), giving their reactions to your presentation. It can be difficult to judge how much the audience has understood at the time of speaking; the *Evaluation form* gives you a better idea of how easy or difficult it was for the listeners to follow what you said. Their detailed comments can be very useful when you are planning future seminars.
2. While the other students are filling in the sheets, *the teacher* talks to you individually, making comments on your performance.

The teacher will then talk to the group as a whole, mentioning points worth general comment (positive or negative), both from your presentation and also from the listeners' contributions at the discussion phase.

A SEMINAR CHECKLIST

Below is a 'checklist' of points to keep in mind as you prepare future presentations. Planning your talks on this basis will help to make you a more confident and effective speaker.

PREPARATION	PRESENTATION	DISCUSSION
Topic – is it appropriate for the audience/occasion? – is it coverable in the time? *Plan* – organisation – structure – point/conclusion *Title* – is it clear? – is it accurate?	*Signposting* – clear enough? *Support material* – handout – flipchart – slides/OHP acetates *Delivery* – speed – word stress *Timing* – allow for reference to handouts, etc. – allow for questions and discussion *Eye contact* – distribution	*Positive attitude* – be patient with questioners *Summarise the question* – for the audience – for yourself *Respond to the question* – answer it – (or avoid answering it!)

Suggestions for further action

There are many different ways in which you can continue to work on your speaking skills after you have completed this book. Here are some suggestions:

Reading

When you come across a key word in a reading text, check its stress pattern – either by asking a native speaker to pronounce it for you or by looking the word up in a learner's dictionary. (Dictionaries for native readers of English are generally less helpful.)

Listening

SEMINARS

Analyse the seminars you take part in. Observe the presentation and assess its strengths and weaknesses in terms of the areas you have practised in *Study Speaking*. Also make a point of listening carefully to the way people ask their questions and whether they manage to make their point clear without needing to repeat it or rephrase it.

INTERVIEWS

Listen to interviews and discussions on radio and TV current affairs programmes. In particular, notice how the interviewer/presenter asks questions and follows them up when the answer is unsatisfactory. Watch for the strategies the interviewees use to avoid answering questions.

Speaking

CONVERSATIONS

Use face-to-face conversations as a means of getting feedback on your spoken English. When you find that your listener finds it difficult to follow what you say, try to identify precisely what has caused the problem. Sometimes the other person will give you a clue as to what they misunderstood or didn't understand, e.g. 'Cartons? Oh, you mean car*toons*' would tell you that incorrect word stress was the problem. If you can't work out what was wrong, ask them to tell you. You may be surprised at the answer – sometimes the actual source of difficulty is not what you might have expected.

SEMINARS

When preparing any sort of presentation, many of us find that it helps to rehearse – not just to read it through but to practise giving the talk aloud as you would in front of an audience. Time yourself; most people underestimate how long the presentation will take. Knowing in advance how much detail to cut out is a great advantage.

Record your rehearsal on cassette. When you play it back, think about possible ways of making the message or the delivery clearer. If you can, get someone else to listen to the tape; they will probably find some points that they have difficulty catching or following.

Make a point of assessing your own presentations. You can use some of the Evaluation questions we have used in the course, to identify the points you might change if you had the opportunity to give the seminar again.

Practice

As with all other skills, the best way to improve is to get the right sort of active practice. Talking to other learners of English can be just as valuable as talking to native speakers – and, since there are more of them in the world, often more convenient! The basic conversational tactics – being prepared to look for an alternative expression, asking the other person to repeat or clarify – are the same no matter who you are talking to.

Paths to communication

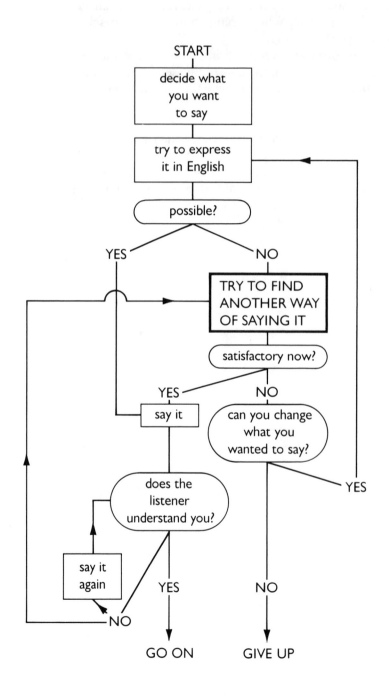

Seminar evaluation form

Complete this form by circling the items in capital letters and by using the spaces below each item for comments or examples that will help the speaker with that aspect of presentation.

1. What do you think were the strengths of the presentation?

2. Were you able to follow the main points?
   YES   WITH DIFFICULTY   NO

3. Would you be able to summarise the talk for someone else?
   YES   WITH DIFFICULTY   NO

4. Was it well-organised?
   YES   GENERALLY   NO

5. Did the speaker indicate when they were moving to a new point?
   YES   GENERALLY   NO

6. Comment on their use of visual aids.

7. Was their speed of speaking appropriate?
   YES   TOO FAST   TOO SLOW

8. Was their voice loud and clear enough?
   YES   GENERALLY   NO

9. Did they give clear explanation of specialist terms?
   YES   GENERALLY   NO

10. What about the quantity of information in the time available?
    SATISFACTORY   TOO MUCH   TOO LITTLE

11. How would you judge the speaker's eye contact with *you*?
    GOOD   POOR

12. If you had other serious difficulties in following the talk, were they caused by:
    ACCENT   GRAMMAR   TOPIC
    others:

13. Did the speaker conclude with a summary at the end of their talk?
    YES   NO

14. How did the speaker deal with questions?
    WELL   SATISFACTORILY   POORLY

15. What advice would you give the speaker for future seminars?

Names

English names normally consist of one or more forenames (usually called 'first names' or 'Christian names') and a surname or family name. They normally occur in that order; it is only in special contexts that the surname is given first, for example, in catalogues, bibliographies and telephone directories. People never introduce themselves as Lynch Tony or Anderson Kenneth, and we also give first name and surname in a formal introduction, not just the surname.

Traditionally, women used to drop their surname ('maiden name') and adopt their husband's surname when they married, although this is now changing. In professional life, especially, it is now common for married women to continue using their own surname.

Which name to use depends on the formality of your relationship with the person you wish to address. Surnames – *always preceded by the appropriate title*, as explained below – are used when talking to adults you do not know well or with whom you have a formal relationship. The first name is used when talking to friends, fellow students, children and colleagues; it is for this reason that we talk about being 'on first-name terms' or 'on Christian-name terms' with someone if we know them well.

In many areas of life in Britain the tendency over the last 30 years or so has been towards less formality in relationships, so it is now common for first names to be used between, for example, academic staff and students or in business or professional contexts. However, the situation varies widely, even between departments in the same university and between different individuals in the same department. The best advice is to pay careful attention to the way other students and staff address each other. When in doubt, it is safer (in Britain) to be more formal rather than less.

Titles

The most usual titles in ordinary life are these:

Mr /mɪstə/ – for men
Ms /məz/ – for women
Miss /mɪs/ – for unmarried women
Mrs /mɪsɪz/ – for married women

The use of the title Ms is increasingly common, particularly in written communication.

There are basically two *academic titles* which can be used in place of the titles above:

Doctor (written Dr) – for people holding a Ph.D. or a medical degree

Professor (written Prof.) – in Britain this is used only for the most senior academic(s) in a university department. The situation is different in the USA and Canada, where *professor* can be a more general term, approximately equivalent to *lecturer* elsewhere.

All titles are used with the *surname alone* when addressing the person, or when referring to someone you know formally:

Mr Anderson   Ms Jackson   Dr Lynch

It is never correct to address someone or to refer to them *by title and first name*. Some foreign learners of English do it, either because they feel it sounds more polite than just the first name, or because they use that form of address in their own language. But the following **would always be wrong**:

Mr Kenneth   Ms Glenda   Dr Tony

It is customary to use *title + initials + surname* (Prof. J. Erickson) on the outside of an envelope and at the top of a letter; however, the letter itself would begin:

Dear Prof. Erickson   or   Dear Jane

depending on how well you knew her.

First name and surname together are often used when introducing people (sometimes preceded by the appropriate title, for clarity):

This is Eric Johnstone   or   This is Dr Eric Johnstone

Surname alone is only used when referring to well-known people, such as scientists ('Einstein') or politicians ('Gorbachev'), but not friends or close colleagues. So you should address people either by **title and surname**, or **first name only**.

Sir/Madam

In Britain, these terms are used only in situations where one person provides a service to another; for example, shop assistants, bank tellers and receptionists might address their customers in this way. In most schools, pupils address teachers as Sir or Miss (regardless of marital status).

Sir and Madam are not generally used in Britain when talking to strangers (unlike, say, North America): they are not used when addressing academic staff.

Transcripts of listening materials

Unit 1

hello / well I've been asked to talk about the course that you're about to embark upon from the perspective of having done the same course last year / so I thought I'd look at three areas that were important for the students on the course last year / obviously I won't cover everything / so do please feel free to add any comments you might have or ask any questions at the end / the three areas I wanted to look at were first of all problems related to adjusting to student life / then the day-to-day workload of the course / and thirdly written assignments the problem of written assignments /

first of all then / adjusting to student life / I don't think anybody should underestimate the importance of getting good accommodation / it's very important I think to make yourself as comfortable as you can / as quickly as possible / because the course only lasts a year / it's not long enough to get a cheap flat and decorate and do the necessary repairs / so most people tended to live in student flats or in university accommodation / halls of residence where you could have your own room and you had the option of eating meals in college or opting out of that and / making other arrangements for food / perhaps eating at the students' union or cooking your own meals / in fact I think some of the people on the course last year who did initially live a little way out of the city / came in / they changed their accommodation and tried to get a room in one of the halls of residence / because they felt happier and more comfortable / and with the heavy commitment that this course does involve it's important to feel relatively free of other worries so you can concentrate on the work /

also I think it was / quite difficult for some of us who had been working for a number of years to adjust to being a student again / and I think this / is also something that you need to consider if you've had your own independence perhaps your own flat / you've been working / to suddenly adjust to being in an academic environment as a student again does take some time / so all these things need consideration and I think it's important as I said to get accommodation that is the best that you can afford so that you're relatively settled and comfortable as quickly as possible /

now then / the second area that I wanted to look at was the business of the actual day-to-day workload of the course / it's a very intensive course / you'll find that you're attending lectures from nine till three or three fifteen / every day of the week / Wednesday and Friday afternoons are supposed to be free but sometimes there are commitments on those days as well / although Wednesday afternoon is officially the university's sports afternoon / so a lot of people like to keep that free so that they could play squash or take part in any other sport that they're interested in / but it is a heavy workload and you find that you have homework most nights / you have assignments to prepare for the next day sometimes / reading to do obviously / so it's very important that you do keep up with the reading if you want to get the best out of the seminars and the lectures / it's useful to buy the set books and you can sometimes get hold of those second-hand from students on last year's course like me / who are often willing to sell them to new students at a discount / otherwise you find you have to rush from lectures straight to the library / to do the reading for the next day / and it is useful if you have at least the basic text / OK so there is quite a heavy workload / at first I think you tend to worry rather a lot and you / take copious notes on all the lectures because you're inevitably worried about missing something important but it does get better after a while and you learn to discriminate / not write everything down / and to trust a bit more to your reading and your own opinions on the subject / so it gets better although at first there does seem to be an awful lot of pressure / but after a while you stop worrying if you miss the occasional lecture as long as you have the readings / and you know / basically the areas that have been covered / but people did manage I think to combine working hard with a social life / you know there is time to do the sort of things that you enjoy in the university or to spend time with your family obviously / 'cause a lot of people were with their families last year / right so if you've got any comments or questions about that perhaps you could mention them when I finish /

now the third area that I wanted to look at was the whole area of written assignments / the course demands five projects of round about five thousand words / and these are assessed and go with the two examination marks and the dissertation to your final mark / and I think at first / particularly with the first project we were really very worried about / about the project and about the marks / you have to wait some time before you get your first marks and I know most of us had absolutely no idea how well or how badly we'd done / but after the first one it gets better and you have a better idea of the standard required / and how you can improve / it was very useful to look at assignments done by students in previous years / because this gave us some idea of what was expected / another point here is presentation / the projects have to be typed or word-processed and bound / and it was very useful to have your own word-processor / your own computer / much less time-consuming than typing / if you've got your own computer too of course you can work on it from the start / and this saves all the time-consuming business of writing first drafts second drafts and final drafts / the university does provide computing facilities and there are classes in word-processing for those who don't know how to use a word-processor / or the particular package that the university uses / and a lot of the students did take advantage of these / which I think were held on a Wednesday

afternoon / so it is really very worthwhile getting into word-processing / I can certainly recommend it rather than typing / some people did pay to have their assignments typed / but it's by no means cheap / and of course you have to be very organised / to get it in at the right time /

OK well I'll stop there / and I'll ask if anybody has any comments or any questions / anything that you'd like to ask me /

(7 minutes 10 seconds)

Unit 2

right I'm going to tell you how British students apply for admission to universities in Britain / that's the students who want to do an undergraduate course leading to a degree such as the B.A. that's the Bachelor of Arts / the B.Sc. the Bachelor of Science / or the M.A. which is the Scottish equivalent to the B.A. /

well first of all there are no separate entrance exams for different universities / except for Oxford and Cambridge / the students in Britain take national school-leaving examinations / now in England they're called A levels and in Scotland they're called Highers / there's a slight difference in these exams / the A levels are slightly more specialised and so people tend to take fewer /

anyway acceptance to a university depends on the number of these exams you have and the grades / and it varies according to each university / I would say at a very rough estimate that you would need about say five Highers for acceptance to a British university / and about / or about three A levels / that's a very rough estimate /

anyway the students choose the universities and the courses that they're interested in by looking at prospectuses / now these are booklets produced by the universities which give information about the courses that they offer / and these prospectuses are available in the schools careers offices / or libraries / or directly from the university /

now all applications are processed through one central body called UCCA / that stands for the Universities Central Council on Admissions / in other words the students don't apply directly to the universities themselves / except for Oxford and Cambridge / they have to apply one year in advance / that is between September and December of the year before the October entry date / you know that the academic year in Britain is from October to June /

well there's one standard form to fill in called the UCCA form / and on this form you put details of your education qualifications any relevant work experience etcetera / plus the exams that you're going to sit during the school year / you also put down a list of the universities that you're interested in / and the courses / and it has to be a maximum of five universities / you can't put them in order of preference / but they're listed according to their code number / the code number is given in the UCCA handbook / however you can mark the university that you strongly prefer /

then you send off the form to UCCA with a fee of six pounds / and once you've sent the form you can't change your list / and by the way you can only send one form per year /

UCCA then sends copies of your application form to the universities on your list / and the universities reply to the student directly / either offering them a firm place / if they meet their requirements / that is they have the right number of exams and grades / or a conditional place / that is acceptance on condition that the students pass the exams that they're going to sit / and at the required grade /

so then the students sit their school exams and they wait anxiously for the results to see if they've met the requirements / and then they let the university know the results / and if they're accepted / they're ready to start in October of that year /

(3 minutes 45 seconds)

Unit 3

so in other words what I'm saying is that / this isn't something that only happens / because you're using a foreign language / even if you're using your own language / certain problems arise in talking with people which need solving / and we get used to doing it in our own language / but it's more of a conscious problem in a foreign language /

OK so what I've done is to put together this / flowchart as you can see / and there are a number of points I wanted to make about it the first thing / you'll see that I've called it 'Paths to communication' / and the title the fact that it says paths / not path / emphasises that *there is always more than one single route to making yourself understood* / and that part of the skill of being a good communicator involves knowing what options to take what alternatives to use /

now you'll see that I've drawn one box with thicker / ink / and the reason for that is that it is in a sense the central box / I think it's the most important part of the process / namely *trying to find another way of saying something* / now there are two possible reasons / why you might need to find an alternative way of saying something / and that's illustrated by the fact that there are two routes into the box / the first reason for needing to find another way of saying something is / that it may be that you can't find / or you can't remember the exact expression in English / for the meaning that you want to / communicate / and the other reason for finding yourself in that box is that / you may have succeeded in finding exactly the right / word or phrase / to convey what you want to say but the person you're talking to may not have understood it / in other words you may find yourself needing to find an alternative expression / either because you have a problem in your own English / or because your listener hasn't understood you /

right oh perhaps I should just mention *some of the options that the speaker has* if you're in that box / and you need to find an alternative way of saying something / well the first thing you might try to do is to find a *synonym* / a word that has the same meaning / just like I did then / another option would be to make an appropriate *gesture* / for example / if you were trying to find the name of an object a thing / you might be able to show the shape of it the height of it and so on / with your hands / the third possibility would be to *translate* / the word that you want / from your own language into another language that the listener speaks / either their first language or / a foreign language that you have in common / you could also *describe* it / say how high it is what it's made of and so on / you could also *paraphrase* / in other words you could say 'well it's a sort of . . .' / or 'it's the sort of feeling you get when . . .' / and you might *explain* / explain what for example the function of the thing was / what it's used for or who uses it / and the final option / would be to *spell the word* / now it may be that you've used the word and the person you're talking to hasn't recognised it and you're fairly sure that it is the right word / sometimes it helps to spell the word aloud / because you may have noticed that quite a few people / when they're using English / because of the difference between the way English is pronounced and spelt / they may not identify words in speech which in fact they would know in writing /

OK from that box / from the central box I'd like to go down to the bottom left-hand corner / and you'll see there that there's the 'say it again' box / now you get into the 'say it again' box because you have answered no to the question 'does the listener understand you?' / one of the things you'll find / perhaps you've noticed already about conversations / where at least one of the people using one of the people in the conversation is using English as a foreign language is that you get this / the speaker says something / the listener doesn't understand it / so the speaker says it again / the listener asks for repetition / speaker says it again and so on / and *they get stuck in a loop* / one of the things I'd say / recommend to you is that if you find yourself down in this left-hand corner / and you've said something again and it still isn't understood / then you need really to go back up towards the central area / in other words *you need to find another way of saying it rather than simply repeating the word* / so you need to be aware of the fact that even if the word you know is right / it may not help the listener simply to repeat it in the hope that they will / understand what the word is /

the last thing I wanted to say was that the whole flowchart / is of course designed from the point of view of the speaker / so the question 'does the listener understand you?' of course / that involves the listener making clear to the speaker that they haven't understood them / so in all this flowchart *the listener too has an important part they have options as well* / if you're the listener and you don't understand what somebody's said / I think there are four main things that you might do four options that you have / first one is to *say that you haven't*

understood / 'I'm sorry I didn't catch what you said' / the second one is to *ask for repetition* / 'sorry could you say that again' or 'would you mind repeating what you just said' / the third one is to *ask for clarification* / it may be that you've understood / the word that they've used / but you don't know what the meaning is / so you've recognised the word as a word / but you don't know what it means / for example let's imagine somebody was talking to you and used the word 'radiator' / and you might say 'well / sorry what do you mean by radiator?' or 'what does radiator mean?' / and the last thing that you might do the last option you have would be to / in the case where you believe you've understood what's being said but you want *to check it* / and one way of doing that is to say / to go back to the case of the radiator / to say something like 'so you mean that I've got to have the radiator repaired?' / or it might mean to say / 'so when you say radiator you mean the part of the heating system?'

so those I think are the main points I wanted to make about the flowchart / as I say it's designed from the point of view of the speaker / but I think one of the most important things about being involved in this complex activity / is the fact that *both partners* / *the listener and the speaker have a role to play* / and usually / if both of them take responsibility for sorting things out it makes it much easier /

(7 minutes 50 seconds)

Unit 4

OK well what I'm going to do is to briefly describe the main differences between English and Outlandic / you should have in front of you / two sets of sentences / with the English on top and the Outlandic underneath / and what I'm going to do is to / explain which bit goes with which bit / in each language and to / try to make clear the main differences between the two languages /

OK so the first sentence 'I have never eaten such a bitter orange' / is in Outlandic 'commay aldri ooma laranja tow azeyda egu' / now to translate that word for word / 'commay' is 'ate' / A T E / 'aldri' is 'never' / 'ooma' is the indefinite article that would be 'a' or 'an' in English / and / 'laranja' is 'orange' / 'tow azeyda' is 'so bitter' / and 'egu' is 'I' / so if we were / to give a word-for-word translation / that would be / 'ate never an orange so bitter I' /

the second sentence / 'she is going there tomorrow evening' / that would be in Outlandic / 'vai imoron di noyt lah zee' / 'vai' for 'goes' / 'imoron' 'tomorrow' / 'di noyt' / you take that together 'di noyt' / is 'at night' / 'lah' is 'there' and 'zee' is 'she' / so the word-for-word translation would be 'goes tomorrow at night there she' /

OK so those are two examples / so what are the main differences / well / the first one / you can see that in the sentences we have 'egu' at the end of the first one / and 'zee' at the end of the second one / so *the subject pronoun comes normally at the end of the sentence* / *in Outlandic* / whereas in English of course / it's at the beginning /

second difference is that / if you look at the / first sentence you have 'such a bitter orange' / in English and 'ooma laranja tow azeyda' / in Outlandic / so you see that the adjective in Outlandic comes before the noun / sorry / *the adjective in English comes before the noun* / *and in Outlandic it comes* / *after the noun* /

the third difference / if you look at the first sentence again / you'll notice there are three / in Outlandic there are three words which all have A / the letter A at the end / 'ooma' 'laranja' / 'azeyda' / and in fact the letter A at the end indicates a feminine noun / so 'laranja' / is feminine and that / causes the / article 'ooma' and the adjective 'azeyda' to agree with it so / one difference between English and Outlandic is that / *in Outlandic you have agreement* / *between articles nouns and adjectives* / and they would all / in the case of a feminine noun they would all end in A /

right so the fourth difference / looking this time at the second sentence you can see that in English we have / 'she's going there tomorrow evening' / but in Outlandic that becomes / 'imoron di noyt' 'tomorrow at night' / so *in Outlandic locative follows temporal* / *for adverbs* /

so / of course those are not the only differences but they are four of the main differences between / the two languages /

(5 minutes 30 seconds)

A   Information tasks

PURPOSE

It would be unrealistic to expect students on pre-session or in-session courses to make their spoken English native-like in the short time available. Our target in *Information tasks* is to help them deploy their resources more efficiently, by focussing their attention on ways of resolving the uncertainties that they are bound to encounter in spoken interaction in English.

Your students may be unfamiliar with the idea of analysing the effectiveness of particular interactional tactics, as we ask them to do, rather than concentrating solely on accuracy. They may be reluctant to accept that *both* parties (listener and speaker) share the responsibility for the successful communication of a message. Some will probably turn to you during a task, saying, 'I don't understand her English' or 'He can't follow what I'm saying' and want to give up. Blaming the other person (explicitly or implicitly) is irrelevant and unhelpful; improving learners' confidence in their ability to *interact* in order to achieve comprehension is at least as important as increasing their language knowledge and control. By reflecting on and talking over the difficulties that arise, they begin to find more effective solutions in two ways – by expanding their language resources and by becoming more resourceful users of English.

PROCEDURE

The basic steps in the teaching sequence are these:
a) set up the task and explain the rules;
b) monitor students' performances;
c) guide their analysis of their problems;
d) provide feedback.

Classroom layout

The *diagram-based* tasks are carried out in pairs. Ideally the students should sit facing their partner with some form of screen (folder, bag, book) placed between them, preventing them from seeing each other's information. In the *'jigsaw-speaking'* activities the students should form a small circle of three or four. For all *Information tasks*, arrange the furniture so as to allow space for you to circulate and listen in to each group, and to minimise the problem of noise interference between pairs/groups.

Step (a): Setting up the task

B versions for tasks 1, 3, 5, 7 and 8 are printed in jumbled order on pages 38–46.
(Page references are given in your Section D *Unit notes*.)

Some instructions are quite complex and it may be necessary to explain unfamiliar
vocabulary in the students' material before they begin their task. However, we
suggest you do *not* pre-teach the language needed to perform the task itself, for two
reasons. Firstly, it would defeat the principal objective of the tasks, namely to create
situations where the learners encounter communication difficulties and gain
experience of message negotiation and repair. Secondly, people are more likely to
learn something when they themselves perceive a need for it; language learners will
benefit more from the teacher responding to their requests for an item of vocabulary
or for a better way of saying something, *once they have themselves tried the task* and
have identified their problems with it.

However, we also include in the *Unit notes* some suggestions for 'Useful
language', to be used selectively if you find it necessary in your particular
circumstances.

Step (b): Task monitoring

It is important to monitor the groups' interaction, not just so as to be able to
comment on faults or weaknesses, but also to make a note of examples of effective
language use in particular performances. Different pairs/groups will vary in how
long they take to complete a particular task; you can take advantage of that to talk
to early finishers about points which you have noted in their performances.

Step (c): Analysis of all problems

An important element in all three Phases is the part of the lesson where the learners
analyse their performance. In the case of the *Information tasks* we provide a
framework in the form of the flowchart *Paths to communication* on page 52. You
may find it helpful, when preparing for the course, to refer to the *Seminar skills*
listening material for Unit 3, which consists of a short talk based on that diagram
(transcript on pages 59–60).

GROUP DISCUSSION

As each group (or pair) completes their task, ask them to think back over their
conversation. Which parts caused them problems? Can they plot the problem on the
flowchart? How did they find their way out of the difficulty? Can they now identify
alternative solutions with the help of the diagram?

CLASS DISCUSSION

When the whole class has finished, collect their comments on the points they have
discussed with their task partner. Write them on the board and elicit suggestions for
solutions to the problems.

Step (d): Feedback

Below we list some common weaknesses in the two principal areas mentioned
earlier: *interaction faults* and *language errors*. For convenience, we refer to the giver
and receiver of information as 'speaker' and 'listener' respectively, although the
'speaker' must of course be prepared to listen and the 'listener' to speak.

INTERACTION FAULTS

Speaker
1. Not giving the listener a general picture of the task ahead.
2. Repeating over and over again a word that has not been understood.
3. Not checking whether the listener has understood.

Listener
The problems we have observed are due mainly to deficiencies in questioning:
1. Not making clear that they haven't understood.
2. Not making clear when a question is a question.
3. Not making clear what the focus of their question is.
4. Not checking that what they have understood is correct.
5. Not being assertive enough, i.e. not persisting with a query.

LANGUAGE ERRORS

Stress
Although students should be aware of which specific sounds they have most difficulty with, the source of real-life misunderstandings of non-native learners' English is often incorrect stress placement, either within a single word or on one part of a sentence. When giving feedback we therefore focus more on stress errors than on phonological errors. (This point is also discussed in *Seminar skills*, Unit 2.)

Spelling aloud
Spelling a word aloud to the listener can be a most efficient way of clearing up ambiguities. If students express surprise that we recommend it, we point out that even native speakers of English resort to spelling to clear up doubts over, for example, 'discrete' and 'discreet' or between 'complementary' and 'complimentary'.

Summary

The *Information tasks* are intended to be problematic and to challenge learners' resources. The materials have been designed to get the students to do three things: (1) to find a way of coping with the difficulties; (2) to reflect on their specific problems in the task and to discuss improvements; (3) to see the applicability of communication strategies to similar situations beyond the classroom.

B Scenarios

OBJECTIVES

Phase 2 is based on the work of Robert Di Pietro (1987), who argues that L2 classroom activities should include practice in coping with situations where there is potential for conflict on a personal level. These *Scenarios* move the spotlight from the factual information transfer of Phase 1 to the achievement of individual goals through persuasion and compromise, where the key to successful performance is flexibility under pressure. All the scenarios in *Study Speaking* are based on actual experiences of our students in Edinburgh.

STRUCTURE

Each scenario involves three stages. In the first ('rehearsal'), the learners are assigned one of two scenario roles and discuss possible routes to their goal. In the second ('performance'), one player from each group performs the scenario in front of the rest of the class, keeping as closely to their group's overall strategy as the opposing player allows. This first performance is followed by group consultation, before two more players perform in a second round. The final stage ('debriefing') gives the class the chance to assess how well the players did and to suggest possible improvements or alternatives.

PROCEDURE

Stage 1: Rehearsal

ARRANGEMENT

Divide the class in half. Assign a role (A or B) to each group and ask the students to read the relevant information. The information for group A is printed in each unit; sets of group B information are printed in jumbled order on pages 38–46. (Page references are given in your Section D *Unit notes*.) The practical maximum number in these groups is eight students; if your class consists of more than 16 learners, it is better to divide them into four groups, with two A groups and two B groups running in parallel at the rehearsal stage. Rehearsal works best if the students in each group form a close circle. This contributes to a feeling of unity and cooperation; it also has the practical advantage that their discussion can be kept confidential.

The main purpose of the rehearsal is for the groups to absorb the background information for their scenario role, to establish their goal and to plan their strategy accordingly. In addition, rehearsal enables the group members to pool ideas and suggestions, reduces anxiety about the coming performance and allows them to learn new language from each other. They also need to choose a player for the next stage.

The A and B role instructions are quite detailed in some cases and learners will need time to take in the information. Some teachers piloting the book felt that the instructions were rather restrictive, limiting the role group to one particular line in the conversation, for example, refusing a request. You can make the roles more flexible by replacing or deleting specific parts of the role instructions, or by encouraging the learners to vary their approach in the two rounds of the performance, adopting, say, a compromising attitude in the first round and a hard line in the second.

When a group asks for assistance at the planning stage, be prepared to give advice, to teach any necessary expressions and to coach their pronunciation, but try to avoid imposing your own ideas on them or giving mini-lectures. The students should get used to relying on each other.

Some suggestions for useful vocabulary are included in the Section D *Unit notes*. As in Phase 1, we recommend that these are not taught in advance, unless a group makes a specific request to which they would be an appropriate response. There is a strong argument for allowing learners to identify a language need for themselves, rather than our assuming gaps in their L2 knowledge and pre-teaching vocabulary to fill them.

Stage 2: Performance

This differs from a theatrical 'performance' in two principal ways. Firstly, the two players are trying to achieve the goals established by their group; they are not enacting a set script. Surprise is a key element. Secondly, the non-performing members of the class are not just an audience; they ought to be involved observers – on the look-out for weaknesses in the strategies of the two players which might be remedied (or exploited) in the second round. It is important to ensure that only the players speak during the performance; if you allow their colleagues to intervene when things go wrong (or differently to what has been planned!) the result can be chaotic.

PROCEDURE

Call the two players out to a position where they can be seen and heard easily. We usually sit them facing each other across a table, rather than expecting them to act it out. One possible advantage of the sitting performance is that if the players are expected to use body movements (e.g. to enter the room, to mime holding or manipulating objects) some may be inhibited by the additional demands of being *actors*, rather than *players* in this particular game.

You will need to record the performance in some way. The simplest method is to make notes on points that you think may be worth commenting on at the debriefing stage. The major advantage of pen-and-paper notes is that they are selective and ready for immediate use; using audio- or videotape makes it more difficult to locate and replay the sequences you wish to comment on. On the other hand, a cassette recording offers a more reliable version of the performance. It would also allow the students to hear or watch themselves at a later stage, e.g. as the basis for individual pronunciation work in the audio- or videolaboratory.

The next step depends on the size of your class. If you divided a larger class into four groups at the rehearsal stage, you can now ask two players from the other A and B groups to perform. If your class consists of only two groups, ask two new A and B players to act out the scenario. **Always try to ensure that there is enough time for a second round of performance**. If not, go straight on to the debriefing.

Stage 3: Debriefing

Di Pietro stresses the need for learners to participate in the evaluation of the performances. Analysis should focus on both content (strategy) and form (language). 'Debriefing' is not just another word for correction by the teacher, although that plays a part.

GROUP DEBRIEFING

After the first performance the groups re-form and discuss. Were their goals achieved? Could they have been achieved more quickly? Did they notice points in the interaction when the other group's player did not understand what was being said? Do they now want to try an alternative strategy discussed at the rehearsal stage?

CLASS DEBRIEFING

After the second round, begin by asking the students for their general reaction to the performances they have seen. The first issue should be the strategies adopted by the two players. Was the outcome what they had expected? Do they feel that there was a 'winner', or was the result a compromise between A and B? Can they suggest any specific actions that might have led to a different outcome?

Those questions are essentially about the *content* of the performances. You should then move on to issues of *form*, the language used by the players. Were any parts of the performance difficult to follow? Did they notice any items of vocabulary or grammar that they would like to comment on themselves, or to have your comments on?

As far as possible, encourage the students to raise points themselves, rather than yourself taking the lead in producing a list of errors that you noted during the performance. Questions often take the form: 'Our player said (X). Is there a better way of saying that?' At this point, you may find it useful to refer to expressions provided in the *Unit notes*.

FEEDBACK FROM THE TEACHER

We give feedback under four headings: Strategy–Information–Communication–Language. In Section E (pages 94–7) you will find a sample scenario performed by two of our students, where we point out the sort of things we would comment on. It may provide some ideas that you can adopt or adapt.

C   Seminar skills

OBJECTIVES

The aim of activities in Phase 3 is to improve students' competence and confidence in five areas of *presentation skills* required for successful performance by the main speaker and three areas of *participation skills* needed in order to make effective contributions as a member of the seminar audience. The sequence of the eight selected skill areas is shown in the *Course map* at the beginning of the book.

DESIGN

The students' materials for Phase 3 are more detailed than for the *Information tasks* and *Scenarios*. Our intention is to make clear the teaching procedure for specific tasks without the need for detailed unit notes in Section D. The basic pattern of work in the *Seminar skills* materials is: Introduction – Preparation – Practice – Presentation – Evaluation/Feedback.

PROCEDURE

Introduction

Work through the lead-in material with the students. Check that they understand the terms used and the point being made. Discussion points should be dealt with first in groups of three to four students and then in plenary; most are intended to provoke an exchange of views rather than to lead to agreement on a correct answer. The *Listening materials* (Units 1–4) are on side 1 of the course cassette; transcripts are provided on pages 57–61.

Preparation

This allows time for individual thought and planning. You may be asked for help with vocabulary or grammar. As far as possible, restrict your advice to *language* points; leave it to the listeners (at the Practice and Presentation stages) to react to and comment on the *content and structure* of their talk.

Practice

For this stage, the students work simultaneously in parallel pairs. Move around the class, noting points for later comment. As in the other Phases, encourage the students to take the initiative in requesting assistance. If it is possible for you to spread the students out into additional rooms or spaces, that reduces problems of noise interference between neighbouring pairs.

Presentation

For this stage, the students should form new groups (trios), since it is essential that each speaker presents their talk to a new audience. As before, the groups work in parallel.

Evaluation/Feedback

Most units contain Evaluation questions specific to the skill being practised. Give students plenty of time to think about their responses *before* you ask them to compare answers. After group discussion, ask for comments from the class as a whole.

Finally, provide feedback on points you have noted at the Practice and Presentation stages which you think are worth bringing to the class's attention – positive, as well as negative. Give priority to points relevant to the specific ground covered in that unit.

TIMING

We have designed the *Seminar skills* activities to take up 90 minutes (or two 45-minute lessons), but you may need to adjust the timing to match your students and your timetable. Below we indicate how, ideally, the distribution of time might work out, assuming two separate lessons of 45 minutes each.

For Units 1–4 (i.e. those *including* a Practice stage):

Lesson 1	*Introduction*	*20–25 mins*
	Preparation	*5–10 mins*
	Practice	*10–15 mins*
Lesson 2	*Presentation*	*25–30 mins*
	Evaluation	*15–20 mins*

For Units 5–8 (i.e. those *without* a Practice stage):

Lesson 1	*Introduction*	*15–20 mins*
	Preparation	*10–15 mins*
	Presentation 1	*15 mins*
Lesson 2	*Presentations 2 and 3*	*30 mins*
	Evaluation	*15 mins*

If your course schedule allows less than 24 hours (for all three Phases), or if your lessons last, say, 60 minutes instead of 45 minutes, you could ask the learners to work through the Introduction and Preparation sections at home. It is in any case an advantage for them to have had the chance to mull over the ideas in advance. Begin the lesson by dealing with their questions about what they have read; then get them to talk over any Discussion points. Using homework in this way may enable you to complete the *Seminar skills* material in one lesson rather than two.

You could also shorten the time spent on the *Seminar skills* work in order to move to the follow-up stage, *Extension work*, where the format changes from group-based mini-seminars to longer presentations to the whole class.

TOPICS

The topics for the speaking tasks in each unit have been chosen to suit a class of students from different countries, though not necessarily from different academic fields, which reflects the classroom mix on many pre-sessional courses. However, we realise that you may be teaching a group who share the same language/culture or the same specialisation, or both. If you find that the topics in the students' material are unsuitable, we offer two suggestions.

Firstly, if the learners come from the same country/culture but from different academic fields, Section D contains an 'alternative topic' for most units. There are two units (5 and 7) where we have found that the original topic in the students' material *is* suitable for a linguistically/culturally homogeneous class.

Secondly, if your students share both first language and academic specialisation, you could get them to base their presentations on a reading text rather than on pre-existing knowledge. They might select an article (not necessarily on a specialist subject), take notes on the main points and use them as a basis for their talk.

With these three basic options you should be able to adapt our materials to suit the needs of your students and the situation you are teaching in.

D   Unit notes

Unit 1   Starting a course

INFORMATION TASK 1: COURSE STRUCTURE

Before starting this first task, show the students the *Paths to communication* flowchart on page 52 (adapted from an interlanguage diagram in Corder, 1981). Its purpose is to raise their awareness of the need to find other communication routes when they experience problems.

Partner B's text is on pages 39–40. As it stands, the lack of information in Partner A's diagram makes this task relatively demanding. To reduce the level of difficulty for your students, you can reveal the contents of one or two of the boxes, e.g. 'Project 2' or 'Examiners' Meeting' (see the solution overleaf).

You may find it helpful to introduce some of the expressions below:

Useful language

Asking for repetition
> *Could you read the bit about practicals again?*
> *Could you repeat what you said about . . .?*

Requesting clarification
> *How do you spell the name of that exam?*
> *So what's the difference between . . . and . . .?*

As Partner B's written text is a *glossary*, most of the academic vocabulary is *defined* in the text, so it should not be necessary for you to explain, for example, what a 'dissertation' or a 'mock' exam are.

Feedback

There are a number of ways of organising feedback on this first activity. One would be to play the class the recordings from the *Sample performances* transcripts 1 and 2, before they try out the 'Course structure' task themselves. This would give them an idea of the sort of thing to look out for in their own performance, for discussion after they have completed the task.

(Although the recordings/transcripts deal with an *Information task* that the learners will be doing in Unit 3, they represent only part of the original performance, so it does not matter if they see the transcripts in advance. There is still plenty of ground for the learners to cover when they try it for themselves in Unit 3!)

Another option would be to record a pair of learners doing the task at the same time as the others, but in a quieter place, such as a corridor or another room. The recording can be played back to the class and discussed (using the flowchart) after all the pairs have completed the task. This has the advantage that everyone can then draw on their own recent experience of doing the task when they analyse and comment on the recorded performance.

Solution

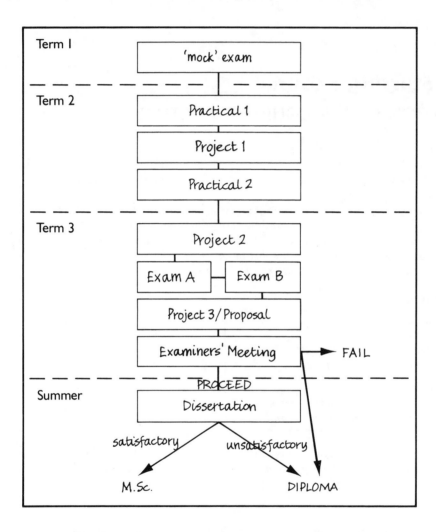

SCENARIO 1: BANK

General notes on procedure are provided in Section B. You will need to explain the ground rules for the scenarios. In particular, it is very important to make it clear that the two players have to perform without any prompts or protests from the other members of their group. Also, remember to allow enough time for a second round of performance.

Group B's information is on page 46. One small language point: use whichever of the names for B's role (*teller* or *clerk*) is more common in the country where the students will be studying.

Useful language

Student
> *I'd like to withdraw . . .*
> *Your colleague must have made a mistake.*
> *Will you accept this . . . as identification?*
> *Can I suggest you phone . . .?*

Teller
> *We don't have an account under your name.*
> *Could you show me . . .?*
> *I'm sure you'll appreciate that we can't . . .*
> *Could you fetch . . .?*

SEMINAR SKILLS 1: SIGNPOSTING

Ask the students to suggest other ways of ordering information, e.g. geographically. Explain the origin of *listener-friendly* (by analogy with *user-friendly*).

Listening

The transcript is on pages 57–8. We suggest you refer learners to it only after they have completed the Discussion points.

Discussion points

Notes:

Introduction
1. Adjusting to student life (accommodation; being a student again)
2. Course workload (reading)
3. Written assignments (look at previous work, presentation/WPing)
Invitation to questions

The other Discussion point questions are open.

Speaking

As the alternative topic (see the note in Section C), the students could prepare a talk on current developments, or an issue of current concern, in their area of specialisation.

Summary

Each unit concludes with a summary, to remind students of the core of the work covered in the unit, particularly if you have had to spread the work over two separate lessons. You can use the summary as the basis for a fuller round-up discussion with the learners.

Unit 2   University systems

INFORMATION TASK 2: STUDENT SOCIETIES

Initial instructions are given in the students' material. As you will see, 'jigsaw speaking' is based on groups of three or four students. All the students receive the same instructions; this page is your source for the materials for the task.

Jigsaw speaking is a variant of the 'strip story' narrative task, but involves two stages of negotiation. First, the groups work out the original sequence of their jumbled sentences, as explained in the students' material. Once a group have reached a solution and have had it checked by you, they then move to a second stage, in which each sentence is dictated in sequence by the relevant 'owner', so that everyone in the group produces a complete written version of the text.

The two stages demand different degrees of precision. Typically, requests for clarification arise at the dictation stage that were unnecessary at the ordering stage, where an overall idea of the content of each sentence may have been enough to solve the problem. (For a detailed rationale, see Lynch, 1983a.)

The base text for the task is as follows:

(B) There are three unions for students at the University of Europe.
(A) Firstly you are automatically a member of the Student Union.
(D) This represents all the students and organises social events.
(B) Secondly, many students choose to join the Sports Union.
(C) Membership entitles you to use facilities, including a gymnasium.
(C) Lastly, if you are studying for a higher degree, you can join the Postgraduate Student Union.
(D) The PGSU is also open to mature students and to graduate research workers.
(A) Remember to take your membership card when you use any of the union buildings.

When preparing the lesson, you should copy, type or write out the sentences on separate strips of paper. To allow the text to be used in groups of three or four, it has been designed so that two sentences can be omitted to make a six-sentence paragraph for trios. The letter in brackets at the start of each sentence indicates the suggested distribution to three (A, B, C) or four (D) students.

We have called the paragraph the *base text* because it can be adapted to suit your students' proficiency level by altering the difficulty of the vocabulary and by raising or lowering the memory load (through the number of items per sentence).

SCENARIO 2: LIBRARY

Group B's text is on page 42.

N.B.   The fact that opening hours are restricted in the current week and that students may not borrow books is the result of a decision by the departmental librarian, not a general university rule. This allows the librarian the option of allowing this one student to borrow, provided it doesn't lead to many more making the same request.

Useful language

> Student
> *I was wondering whether I could . . .*
> *If I could just explain the problem . . .*
> *I know you're busy but . . .*
> *I'm afraid that would be too late for me to . . .*
>
> Librarian
> *I see your problem, but . . .*
> *If I make one exception . . .*
> *Couldn't you . . .?*
> *Why not . . .?*

SEMINAR SKILLS 2: DELIVERY

Discussion point 1

The main-stressed syllables are underlined: oc<u>cur</u>, <u>pur</u>pose, tech<u>nique</u>, aca<u>dem</u>ic, deve<u>lop</u>ment, e<u>vent</u>, <u>con</u>centrate, <u>pro</u>cess.

If necessary, tell the students that the phonemic transcription provided in most EFL dictionaries also indicates the main-stressed syllable; they may be unaware that the information is available there. It is probably more cost-effective to encourage students to make a point of checking the dictionary entries for key items in their talks, rather than trying to provide them with 'rules' (or even regularities) of word stress in English.

Discussion point 2

Possible implications of placing the main sentence stress on various words (underlined) would be: <u>A lot</u> = not a few; <u>overseas</u> = but not local; <u>undergraduates</u> = but not graduates; <u>applied</u> = but not yet been accepted; <u>Diploma</u> = but not the other courses.

Further practical material to help students to recognise and interpret sentence stress is available in Unit 3 of *Study Listening* (Lynch, 1983*b*) and *Elements of Pronunciation* (Mortimer, 1976).

Discussion point 3

The student seemed to ignore the two-way nature of communication, of which 'speaking' is only one part. This point is made again in the unit summary.

Listening

Get the students to tell you the steps in the process. Collect this information on the board and then confirm it with the transcript on pages 58–9. See if they have understood what *UCCA* stands for and what the difference is between *Highers* and *A levels*. Offer clarification of any points they want to know more about. Ask if they can suggest ways in which the speaker might have made the talk clearer. (Enumeration of the stages in the process is one possibility.)

Speaking

For the alternative topic, we suggest that students plan a talk on entry into, and promotion in, their profession: accepted initial qualifications, recognised types of experience, routes to advancement, promotion opportunities, their own ambitions, etc.

Summary

Although we have de-emphasised the problem of segmental pronunciation, you may wish at this point to ask your students to say which English sounds they encounter particular problems with. However, we suggest you close the unit by saying that whatever their problems in producing the sounds of English, they will be more easily understood if they get stress right and if they speak slowly enough to allow listeners the time to adjust to their individual accent.

Unit 3 Accommodation

INFORMATION TASK 3: LAYOUT OF A FLAT

Partner B's information is on pages 43–4. Remember that this task is featured in transcripts 1 and 2 in Section E, so you might wish to use those recordings either before or after your students do the task themselves.

The task is made easier if the two partners discuss first what overall approach they want to adopt. Most listeners find it helpful if the speaker gives them a *general picture* of the layout before launching into details about the precise location of walls and doors. You could point this out to the students in advance; alternatively, you may wish to leave it until the feedback stage. We find that the 'general-picture-first' pairs have less difficulty and complete the task quicker, which we then use as a starting point in follow-up discussion.

Useful language

a vertical/horizontal line	*hall/corridor*
the door opens inwards to the right	*(prepositions)*
the outside wall	*L-shaped*
about one-third of the way up/down/along . . .	

Notes

1. Some piloting teachers reported that this task was difficult for their students. Listening to the *Sample performances* first will help you to assess its complexity relative to the level of the learners in your class. Two possible ways of making the task less demanding are: (a) tell A partners the position of the kitchen/dining room, which then acts as a reference point for the other rooms in the flat; (b) pre-teach or revise some of the vocabulary you think will assist them.
2. For some people, instructions on this type of task are easier to follow if they are given in real-world terms (e.g. 'draw a wall between the outside wall and the corridor') rather than in geometrical terms ('draw a horizontal line from the left-hand vertical line to the first vertical line on the right').

3. The two basic strategies for this sort of location task are: (a) to describe a *route* through the flat, i.e. 'you go in the front door and the first room on your left is . . .'; (b) to talk in terms of an *overview*: 'top . . ., bottom . . ., left . . ., right . . .'. The first runs the risk that, although the speaker may realise that left and right change as you follow the mental route, some listeners do not.

SCENARIO 3: STUDENT ACCOMMODATION OFFICE

Group B's text is on pages 42–3.

Useful language

> Officer
> *Well, you have to realise that . . .*
> *I'm afraid there's not really very much more I can do for you.*
> *I could give you a list of agencies.*
>
> Student
> *I hope I'm not being a nuisance.*
> *I really do need to find a flat nearer to . . .*
> *How soon would I be able to move in?*
> *That's more than I can afford.*

SEMINAR SKILLS 3: USING VISUAL AIDS

Discussion point

Board (white, black, felt, magnet); wall (wallcharts, maps, posters); paper (handout, flipchart); acetate (photographic slide, overhead projector transparency); magnetic tape (videocassette) or disk (projected computer display screen); model (e.g. DNA structure). Relative (dis)advantages will include availability, cost, flexibility and dependence on technology.

Listening

Ask the students to compare their notes and to ask you to explain points that they have not fully understood. When they have done that, they can be referred to the transcript on pages 59–60, where the main points are in italics.

Ask them for their comments on the relationship between the presentation and the visual aid. Did the speaker's talk *explain* parts of the flowchart? Did he *add* information not given there? Did they find he allowed them enough time to take in the points he was making?

Speaking

For the alternative topic, the students might describe a complex process or procedure in their field of work. It is important to select a subject that they know their listeners will not be familiar with. It should also be one that can be accompanied by an appropriate visual aid.

Useful language

> As you can see on the map (diagram/graph), . . .
> If you look at the map (etc.), you'll see . . .
> What this map (etc.) shows is . . .
> On this map (etc.), X stands for / represents . . .

Unit 4   Language

INFORMATION TASK 4: LANGUAGE LEARNING

For guidelines on this activity, see the notes for Unit 2. The additional difficulty built into this task is that one sentence – here, the topic sentence – is withheld, for the groups to work out.

Base text
(X) Learning a foreign language can be frustrating.
(A) It is clear that some people find it much more difficult than others.
(B) The more successful ones seem to adopt various common principles.
(C) Firstly you should accept that you are going to make mistakes.
(A) They are inevitable and necessary if you are going to make any progress.
(C) You also have to be flexible and resourceful when problems arise.
(B) In conversation, for example, you may need to repeat or explain.
(D) A third principle is to seek as much active speaking practice as possible with native speakers.

As before, the letters in brackets indicate the sentences for distribution to a group of three learners (A,B,C) or four (A,B,C plus one longer sentence for learner D). X indicates the sentence which is *not* given out and whose content the students should work out on the basis of the logic and cohesion of their agreed sequence. You can adjust the task on the lines suggested in the Unit 2 notes, if the students found the previous jigsaw task too easy or difficult.

SCENARIO 4: LANGUAGE COURSES

Group B's text is on page 41.

Useful language

> Student
> > I'm sorry to bother you, but I wanted to ask about . . .
> > I'm worried about . . .
> > I really don't feel that my . . . is good enough.
> > After all I only got just over 60.
>
> Course director
> > The problem is that . . .
> > Have you any reason to think you have serious language problems?
> > Instead of coming to classes, why not . . .?
> > You would do better to . . .

SEMINAR SKILLS 4: GETTING CLARIFICATION

Listening

The talk is based on a comparison of two sentences in English and Outlandic. Write up the two sentences (in both languages) *before playing the cassette*. The learners should write them down with plenty of space between Sentences 1 and 2 for their notes.

Sentence 1:

> English: *I have never eaten such a bitter orange.*
> Outlandic: *Commay aldri ooma laranja tow azeyda egu.*

Sentence 2:

> English: *She is going there tomorrow evening.*
> Outlandic: *Vai imoron di noyt lah zee.*

As they hear the talk, the students take notes on the main differences between the two languages. The four mentioned are in italics in the transcript on pages 60–1.

The speaker's explanation of the fourth difference (that in Outlandic time adverbials come before place adverbials) is intentionally unclear. The students should therefore need to ask you for clarification.

Speaking

Alternative topic: two different approaches to an issue, or two possible solutions to a problem, in the student's specialist area.

Summary

This reminds learners of the need for both participants to take responsibility for clearing up uncertainties, in order to improve the efficiency of communication, especially where the purpose of the interaction is the transfer or exchange of information.

Unit 5   Teaching

INFORMATION TASK 5: DEPARTMENTAL ORGANISATION

Partner B's diagram is on page 41. By filling in only one segment of it, we have designed this task to be relatively difficult. To make it simpler, you could reveal the labels for one or more of the other segments, e.g. 'tutors/supervisors' in the postgraduate course third of the disc.

Solution

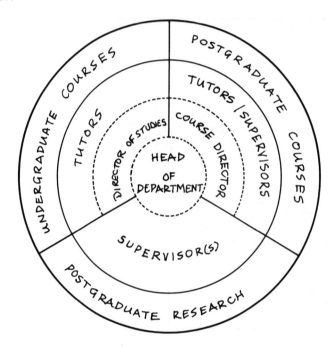

This task may lead on naturally to questions and class discussion as students compare their own systems with the (British) one shown in the diagram. If some pairs finish the *Information task* ahead of others, you could set them the following puzzle:

Academic rank

The five basic academic ranks in British university departments are reader, professor, assistant lecturer, lecturer, and senior lecturer. Not all lecturers are professors; all professors are lecturers. What is the correct order of seniority?

(Solution: professor – reader – senior lecturer – lecturer – assistant lecturer.)

SCENARIO 5: POSTPONING AN ESSAY

Group B's information is on page 38.

Useful language

> Student
> *Is there any chance of getting an extension for this essay?*
> *I realise that it would be inconvenient, but . . .*
> *I know I have already had an extension but . . .*
> *I really did everything I could to get hold of the book but . . .*
>
> Tutor
> *This* is *the second time you've . . .*
> *But it's a question of fairness . . .*
> *You should have had plenty of time to . . .*
> *Why didn't you come to tell me about this earlier?*

Note: As we stress in the section on *Names*, students will encounter wide variation between departments and individuals on the issue of expected/accepted forms of address.

SEMINAR SKILLS 5: QUESTIONING

Discussion point 1

Possible reasons: (a) to check that you have understood the question properly; (b) to ensure that other members of the audience, who often cannot hear what the questioner has said, know what it is about; (c) to give yourself more time to think of an answer.

Discussion point 2

A higher risk alternative would be for the speaker to say something on the lines of *That's not something I've thought about, but perhaps you would like to give your view?* This means the questioner has the right/duty to comment, but the speaker risks losing face.

Discussion point 3

This draws attention to the way in which – in Britain – the adverbs *really, perhaps, in fact, slightly, actually* and the phrase *I think* all act as 'hedges', reducing the directness of the criticism. However, they might be inappropriate for the cultural context your students will be studying in.

Speaking

At the Presentation stage in the last four units of the course, you will need to keep a careful eye on the clock. Each speaker is allowed up to ten minutes for their talk and a further five minutes for questions. This makes a minimum of 45 minutes for each trio to complete the Presentation stage. (See the notes on timing in Section C.)

When the students are dealing with questions from their two listeners, remind them to repeat or summarise the question before answering it. You (and they) may be surprised by the differences that emerge at this point between what was asked and what is understood.

The same 'course methods' talk should also be suitable even if the students share the same subject specialism, since the task requires them to discuss their personal perceptions/opinions of a course they have attended.

Unit 6   Health

INFORMATION TASK 6: MEDICAL TREATMENT

For guidelines on this activity, see the notes for Units 2 and 4. The additional factor of difficulty built into this task is that the sentence you withhold from the students is not the topic sentence, unlike Unit 4.

Base text
(C) All students in Britain used to receive medical treatment free of charge.
(A) Now the regulations covering foreign students have been changed.
(C) Only students doing a course of at least six months are considered 'temporary residents'.
(B) This entitles them to exemption from health service charges.
(A) Their immediate dependants (spouse and children) are also exempted.
(X) Students who are on a course lasting less than six months have to pay for treatment.
(D) Such students are therefore strongly advised to take out health insurance for themselves and their dependants.
(B) Charges do not apply in the case of accident and emergency treatment.

Again, the bracketed letter indicates the sentences for distribution to either a three-student group (A,B,C) or a four-student group (A,B,C plus the longer sentence for D). X is the sentence whose content the groups have to work out on the basis of their agreed sequence.

   If necessary, change the task on the lines suggested in the notes for Unit 2, according to your students' performance on the two previous jigsaw tasks. Adapt the content to match the situation in the country where your students are – or will be – studying.

SCENARIO 6: DOCTOR'S SURGERY

Group B's text is on page 40.

Useful language

Student
I'm sorry to take up your time again . . .
It's not getting any better.
a sharp/dull pain
Perhaps I didn't describe the symptoms very well.
Doctor
How's the stomach?
Any vomiting?
The medicine may take a few days to have an effect.
It's quite usual to get these symptoms when you're tense.
I'm quite sure there's nothing to worry about.

SEMINAR SKILLS 6: NON-VERBAL SIGNALS

Discussion points 1–3

Responses to the questions in these three Discussion points will vary according to where the learners are from. Our students have found this particular discussion enjoyable and enlightening – although not all of them have been willing to accept that the interpretations of gestures in different cultures are equally 'logical'. You need to be diplomatic in eliciting the differences.

Discussion point 4

Psychologists say that eye contact acts as a means of cementing the social relationship and as a channel of communication. So taking option (d) could have the positive effect that everybody feels they are getting individual attention. However, there is a risk that in making a conscious effort to distribute eye contact as equally as possible among the listeners, we end up doing it too mechanically, 'sweeping' the audience from left to right and back again like a radar dish.

The most effective and least obvious strategy may be to try to remember to look at different individuals at different points in the presentation. This is not easy; most of us tend to pick out one person in the group – for example, one who happens to nod or to look interested early on – and continue to direct our gaze at them.

Discussion point 5

We believe the assessment *was* influenced by eye contact.

Speaking

Alternative topic: to describe the methods, results, etc. of a project or study that they have worked on.

Unit 7   Evaluation

INFORMATION TASK 7: TRAVEL GRANT COMMITTEE

This task is the great-grandchild of one in Ur (1981). It is designed for groups of three or four students, whose reading material is distributed as follows: Reference 1, page 44; Reference 2, page 40; Reference 3, page 42; Reference 4, page 38. The intention is to get learners to evaluate the relevance of qualifications and experience.

It consists of two stages: *information transfer* and *discussion*. The first stage requires each student to summarise, rather than to give a dictation. As before, encourage the listeners/notetakers to ask for clarification and repetition as necessary. The second phase will involve a series of decisions, from agreeing on the criteria for selection to settling on a final choice of applicant.

Useful language

> *We have to agree on criteria first.*
> *Should we take (age) into account?*
> *I don't see that (X) is relevant.*
> *I'm not sure about that.*
> *Are we agreed, then?*

Note: The issue of the first postgraduate year, mentioned in Reference 3, also comes up in Scenario 8. In some universities, students intending to do a Ph.D. spend an initial year 'on probation'. Towards the end of that year, they present a proposal to a research committee including their supervisor. If the proposal is accepted, the student is promoted to a full Ph.D. student; if not, they may be asked to revise and re-submit the proposal, or advised to register for a lower qualification such as an M.Phil.

SCENARIO 7: EXAMINATION RESULTS

Group B's information is on page 44.

Useful language

> Student
>   *I had a feeling it wouldn't be very good.*
>   *I think there are probably a number of reasons for it.*
>   *I've probably spent too much time on . . .*
>   *I do realise I'm going to have to . . .*
>
> Supervisor
>   *I'm afraid your result wasn't too good.*
>   *You seem to be having some problems with . . .*
>   *To be honest, we're worried about your work.*
>   *There's a real risk that . . .*
>   *We feel that you should go to the English language classes.*

SEMINAR SKILLS 7: CONCLUDING

Discussion point 1

The speaker could have indicated the main headings or points at the start of their talk, in a number of ways: by showing a projector slide or transparency of the main headings; by giving them to listeners on a handout; by writing them up on the board. Any of these methods could now be used again to provide a visual summary of the ground covered.

Discussion point 2

The third is the only one that doesn't suggest that the speaker has overrun their time; it might be the best from the point of view of making a good impression. Many speakers do finish weakly, e.g. (a), (b) or (d), or even with something as brief as '*OK – any questions?*'

Speaking

Make sure that the student trios keep to the procedure suggested for Stage 2: the three talks, each followed by questions, and *then* general discussion of the issue. (Otherwise you may find that talks 2 and 3 are pre-empted by discussion of talk 1.) The Evaluation stage then follows their general discussion. We have not suggested an alternative topic for this unit; in our experience, the issue of written exams causes natural differences of opinion in the most homogeneous groups!

Unit 8   Research

INFORMATION TASK 8: RESEARCH TRENDS

Partner B's information is on page 45.

1. The main areas of difference are the growth in information science from 0.4% to 21.9%, and the fall of social sciences from 28.5% to 11.6%.
       N.B. The students ought to realise that it is not possible to compare the figures for total expenditure as they stand, since they do not allow for the effect of inflation over the decade 1977–87. When adjusted, the 1987 figure is approximately £31 m at 1977 prices; in other words, there was no significant change in real terms in total expenditure on research.
2.–3. Perhaps a pie chart or a bar graph, showing percentages. A line graph would be inappropriate without data on the intervening years 1978–86.
4. You may need to revise or teach expressions of inference (*might/could/may/ must have* . . .). Two possible reasons for the changes: information science became more important because of technological advances in the 1980s; social sciences were not a priority for the Thatcher government that came into office in 1979.

The completed table:

Government research grants to postgraduates at UK universities in 1977 and 1987				
	1977	%	1987	%
Biological sciences	1 832	15.9	1 974	16.4
Chemistry	1 444	12.5	1 599	13.2
Information science	51	0.4	2 639	21.9
Mathematics	692	6.0	673	5.6
Physics	1 050	9.2	584	4.8
Social sciences	3 285	28.5	1 402	11.6
Others	3 175	27.5	3 201	26.5
Total	11 529	100.0	12 072	100.0
Total expenditure	£30 m		£71 m	

(*Based on the Central Statistical Office* Annual Abstract of Statistics 1989, *London: HMSO*)

SCENARIO 8: RESEARCH PROPOSAL

Group B's information is on page 43.

Useful language

> Student
> *I don't think the committee have been very fair with me.*
> *There are several things that I think you ought to know.*
> *If I had had more contact with my supervisor . . .*
> *This is very serious for me personally.*
>
> Head of Department
> *I do sympathise but . . .*
> *Your proposal just isn't strong enough.*
> *I'm afraid that's beyond our control.*
> *Let me explain what the committee have recommended.*

SEMINAR SKILLS 8: DISAGREEING

Discussion point 1

We would expect (British) students to be less formal and to ask more questions if the speaker were one of their peers.

Discussion point 2

Perhaps the overseas students (a) understood less and therefore asked more, (b) lacked the *language* to disagree and asked questions instead, or (c) felt *culturally* uncomfortable disagreeing. Alternatively, the finding could be due to chance.

Discussion point 3

Additional expressions: simply *But . . .; I take your point, but . . .; But all the evidence suggests that . . .*

Speaking

As stated in the students' material, the choice of topic is to be agreed between the learners and yourself.

After the usual three stages, the students look at the *Seminar evaluation form* on pages 53–4. You will probably need to clarify some of the items. Overall, its function is to elicit individual listeners' impressions of the presentation; it is not designed to be objective.

The spaces below each question allow the listener to comment on specific examples of things that they felt were inadequate (or particularly good). Our students have found it more useful to be given detailed responses than to receive feedback only in the form of circled items.

You can photocopy the two pages of the *Evaluation form* for use in later sessions, e.g. in *Extension work*. It has been designed so that it can be copied onto both sides of a single A4 sheet.

Extension work

When the students have decided on topics and titles for their seminars, draw up a list of speakers, titles and dates. Copies can be given to each student and posted on the class noticeboard.

Preparation

Work through the *Extension work* notes on pages 47–9, explaining and expanding as necessary. Draw the learners' attention to two sections in particular: 'Planning' on pages 47–8 and the 'Checklist' of points on page 49.

Procedure

PRESENTATION

Keep a strict eye on the clock and if the speaker has not finished by the end of their allotted time, ask them to wind up.

QUESTIONS/DISCUSSION

Only comment at this stage if there is a serious breakdown of communication. This tends to occur, as we said in Units 4 and 5, when the speaker misunderstands a listener's point and answers a different question.

EVALUATION

The notesheet that we use during the presentation and discussion phases is shown on page 88. You are welcome to adapt or adopt it for your own teaching.

Talk to the presenter out of earshot of the other learners; this reduces possible embarrassment on their part and avoids influencing what the other students write on their *Evaluation forms*.

When you have talked to the presenter, collect in their forms. Go through the points of general interest from your notesheet. After discussion (or at the end of the class) hand over the listeners' forms to the presenter.

Alternatives

For practical reasons you may prefer to offer different sorts of further practice than we have suggested here. Our EAP course timetable consists of 90-minute sessions, so our *Extension work* is based on two 45-minute modules. If you have more time at your disposal, you will be able to arrange seminars featuring longer main presentations.

On the other hand, the difference between a shorter and a longer seminar is relatively superficial. The experience of putting into practice the skills covered in the eight units can probably be achieved as well in a 15-minute presentation as in a longer one. Once you can give a competent and confident presentation in a foreign language, its actual length is relatively unimportant.

Notesheet

PRESENTER	AUDIENCE
Structure	Non-comprehension
Visual aids	Clarification
Signposting	Questions
Eye contact	Disagreeing
Conclusion	

LANGUAGE	
Vocabulary	Grammar
Stress	Speed

E Sample performances

This section is intended to give you an idea of: (1) what sort of performance to expect on the three types of task in the course, and (2) how we would respond to them when giving feedback. As the title suggests, the samples are taken from classroom recordings, and should not be thought of as models. In transcribing the speakers' words, we have omitted some natural hesitations.

To the right of the speakers' words are examples of the comments we make to students when playing back recordings like these. As you will see, they include positive points as well as criticisms, as it is important to focus on instances of effective use of language, and not simply to encourage learners to look for weaknesses and errors.

You will probably find other points that you would comment on, particularly in the case of pronunciation. In deciding which errors to mention, our principal concern is whether the mistake caused (or is likely to cause) a misunderstanding. Not all errors matter communicatively and part of the teacher's job is to select which ones to focus on and which to leave. As we explained at the start of the book, we regard it as unrealistic to expect students – most of whom are not specialists in English – to produce native-like sounds; what we aim to do is to help them to be effective non-native communicators.

INFORMATION TASKS

We recorded two pairs performing the flat layout task from Unit 3. In each case, what you hear and see is the first four minutes of conversation, which is probably enough to illustrate the overall differences between them and to indicate why one pair was more successful than the other.

Transcript 1

The 'speaker', N(athalie), is from Belgium; the 'listener', F(aris), comes from Iraq.

N *well when you enter the flat what you find* directly on your left hand is the boxroom but you can't enter the boxroom by this way just have this is a room called the boxroom you have to enter the lounge which is straight ahead of the main door . . . (and the door) of the lounge opens towards the right OK

N goes straight to detail; she provides no general picture of what F is to expect, which leaves him 'in the dark'. She does not make clear that there is a hall/corridor.

F yeah

N when you are into the lounge you go *till the . . . right* of the L and at the end of it going to the . . . going up a bit you can find the door of the boxroom open . . . towards the left

'right' may be ambiguous – right as F looks at the plan, or right from the point of view of someone in the lounge?

F *you mean lunchroom living room? yes? this is when you are coming when you are entering to the flat*

F asks for confirmation but gets none.

N no not directly you can't enter directly into the lounge

F but there is a doorway something like a small door a small room called doorway

N it isn't called doorway but I think it's like a door yeah you know . . . *a passage*

= hallway, corridor

F yes

N which . . . drives you up to the other rooms

F yes yes yes

N hm?

F hm . . . that's on the right hand yes

N on the right hand

F on the right side

N when you enter yes it is

F yes

N and um . . .

F *how many rooms?*

F now signals that he needs a general picture, but N does not answer his question. Did she hear it? Did she understand it? F should have persisted until he got a response.

N well the lounge is about two-thirds of the small part of the L no

F yes

N and then the boxroom it begins at the end of the main door and it follows you know it goes . . . it goes on the lounge

F *yes*

N if you see what I mean

F *yes yes yes*

'yes' appears to indicate that F has understood, but his eventual drawing (see opposite) shows that he could not follow adequately. He should have made it clear that he was in difficulty.

N and then the door is at the end of this wall

F yes

N the door of the boxroom

F OK

N OK?

F OK

N then when you enter the flat if you are turning directly at your right there is a long corridor

F yes

N *which leads to first the kitchen then the bedroom the bathroom and to another kitchen*

It would have helped if this information had been given earlier.

F please . . . the kitchen firstly the kitchen . . .

N which is . . .

F which is on the

N right near the lounge

F yes

N next to the lounge

F the kitchen and . . .

N then you have a bedroom

F yes

N then a bathroom and then another bedroom

F another bedroom

N yeah

F yes

N there are two

F *maybe here . . . OK and . . . that's all?*

Is this a question to N? F seems uncertain but does not ask N for additional help.

N um . . .

F what about . . .?

(4 minutes)

Their conversation continued for another five minutes or so, before they got into real difficulty and were advised to stop. Here is what F's layout looked like by then:

F and N's difficulties were in part caused by weaknesses in three areas that we have drawn attention to in the transcript:

1. It helps to give (and to be given) a general picture of the task first.
2. Each partner needs to listen and respond to the other. To some extent, F and N were talking 'past' each other, not reacting to the other's contributions. This can happen in information-gap tasks, where Partner A concentrates so intently on their side of the task that they do not notice the signals of difficulty coming from the listener.
3. It is not enough simply to recognise (as F did) that you are having problems in making sense of what you are being told; you also have to make those problems clear to the speaker, so that they can adjust their message. At various points, F asked questions that might help him to sort out the information N had given him, but he did not persist (perhaps out of politeness, or shyness) with the questions he had started.

Transcript 2

Here, the 'speaker' is M(auro) from Italy; the 'listener' is E(ndang) from Indonesia.

M (this is a) double . . . *double bedrooms flat*   = *two-bedroomed flat*
E   yes

M   there's a bathroom between the two bedrooms a kitchen a lounge and a boxroom

E   can you tell me where is the bedroom the two bedroom?

M   could you repeat please?

E   can you tell me where is the two bedroom?

M   oh . . . we are just on the main door and we are coming in

E   hmhm

M   you turn right

E   turn right yes

M   and you will find you are going to find a bedroom just to your left side to your left then you walk *ahead*

E   you . . .?

M   you walk ahead and you'll find the bathroom on your left

E   *on left side?*

M   pardon?

E   *if I come through the main door I find bedroom on left side?*

M   oh . . . we are *on* the main door

E   hmhm

M   you have to turn

E   turn right

M   right

E   hmhm

M   and you are going towards the up . . . the up side of the . . . the flat

E   hmhm

M   on your map so we are on the night part of the flat we have the first bedroom the bigger on our left then we are going to find a bathroom

E   excuse me can you repeat again?

M   first

E   first . . . the bedroom

M   first the bedroom

E   hmhm

M   second the bathroom third just in front of you

E   hmhm

M   the bedroom the smaller one

E   hmhm . . . on left side yeah?

M   now . . . *if you think to be on the main door* again

E   hmhm

M   you are going to find the lounge just in front of you

E   just in front of me

M   yeah?

E   if I come back the main door hmhm

M   and the kitchen

E   *and the kitchen . . . is the dining room*

M   *in the corner of our L flat*

E   *ah it's the dining room*

M   *kitchen and dining room*

E   *kitchen and dining room*

Here (unlike in the first transcript) the speaker (M) does begin by giving a general idea of the complete plan. But he does not make clear that's what he's doing. When E asks him where the bedroom is, he appears to be diverted ('oh . . .') from his general strategy into giving details. Good original intention, though.

= *straight ahead*

Apparently M is going too fast for E. If M realises that, he should offer to repeat. If he doesn't, E should ask him to slow down.

= *by, at*

= '*If you imagine you're by the main door*'

Compare what the two partners think the other *means by looking at E's version of the plan (opposite).*

M and if you are thinking to be on the main door
    again
E hmhm
M you have the boxroom just on your left
E *boxroom?*
M boxroom OK? this has concerned the layout
    of . . . each room now I'm going to describe you
    the position in which you can find doors and
    windows

(4 minutes)

*A good example of an ambiguous question. Is E
asking M to say where the boxroom is, to explain to
her what a boxroom is, or is she repeating it to
herself, rather than wanting an answer? Whichever it
is, M does not ask what she means.*

M and E continued for a further seven minutes, in a cooperative way, with E asking
for repetition and clarification when necessary and M generally repeating and
rephrasing in line with her requests. By the end of their conversation (11 minutes in
total), E's flat plan was creditably similar to the original:

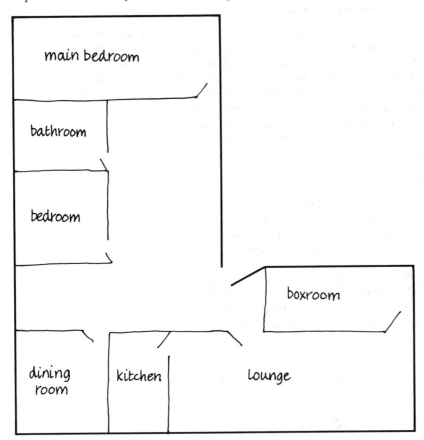

This second performance illustrates the benefits of more supportive talk than we saw
in transcript 1. By making clear when she had comprehension problems, and what
they were caused by, E elicited helpful information from M. However, there were
points in their conversation where greater clarity would have helped: M could have
said, 'Before you start drawing, I'll give you a general idea of what the whole flat
looks like'; towards the end, the confusion over the relationship between kitchen
and dining room might have been avoided if M had described them as 'together' or
'combined' or 'both in one room'. But, overall, this was a good performance.

SCENARIO

In assessing scenario performances, we ask ourselves the following questions, broken down into four broad areas (from most important to least important):

STRATEGY   Did they manage to get what they wanted?
                Did one player come off the loser?

INFORMATION   Did they use relevant role information provided?
                Did they forget or change any details?

COMMUNICATION   Were there any breakdowns in communication?
                How (and how well) did they resolve them?

LANGUAGE   Did they appear to manage to express their intended meaning?
                Did their performance reveal any significant gaps in grammar, vocabulary or pronunciation?

In practice, these four categories of question are sometimes interrelated. For example, a student might pronounce a word in such a distorted way (LANGUAGE) that it was not understood, but the two partners in the conversation might then cooperate in clearing up the difficulty (COMMUNICATION). But for the purpose of providing learners with feedback, we separate our comments into the four categories shown above. (In the transcript, we have abbreviated them to STRAT, INFO, COMM and LANG.)

The players in the recording are J(ulia) from China and T(om) from Japan. They are playing a hotel scenario, which they prepared for in the way explained in Section B. Their role instructions were as follows:

Group A: Hotel guest

You arrived in Britain last night on your way to begin a university course. You stayed overnight at a small hotel. You have to leave by 7.30, as you have to be at your country's Educational Attaché's Office in London by 9 a.m. You have £40, but will be collecting more from the Office today.

It is now 7 a.m. and you have asked the hotel receptionist for the bill, which is for £32 for room with bath, including breakfast. In fact you were unable to use the shower this morning, as there was only cold water. The hotel does not serve breakfast before 7.30.

The price list in your room showed that the price for a room without bath is only £25. You object to paying for a shower that you did not use and for breakfast that you cannot have. The receptionist has gone to get the assistant manager. How will you persuade them to reduce the price?

Group B: Assistant manager

It is the low season and your hotel has recently reduced the number of staff. The prices have also been cut and are now as follows:

Double room with bath/shower £45.00 per night
Double room without bath/shower £36.00 per night
Single room with bath/shower £32.00 per night
Single room without bath/shower £25.00 per night

The single rooms without bath/shower are cheaper because they are very small and do not have a view.

The receptionist has asked you to deal with a guest who has

complained about not having been able to use the shower in their room. As an economy measure, hot water is available only after 7.00 a.m.

The General Manager comes on duty at 8 o'clock and you prefer not to deal with guests' complaints yourself. How can you persuade the guest to wait?

Transcript 3

J   good morning can I speak to your assistant manager please?

T   yeah I'm assistant manager

J   oh well yeah OK I've got a little bit problem

T   right what?

J   *and I would like to discuss you with the . . . with the bill*   COMM. *Successful interactive 'repair'.*

T   *the . . . ?*

J   *with the bill which I*

T   *bill*

J   *yeah I'm going to pay the*

T   *OK*

J   *the bill*

T   *yeah*

J   I feel it a bit unfair

T   yeah

J   because according to the bill I'm going . . . I have to pay the 32

T   32

J   pounds

T   yeah

J   for the room with a bath including breakfast

T   OK

J   *but actually I couldn't have breakfast because*   COMM. *Successful repair.*

T   *you couldn't?*

J   *I couldn't have breakfast*

T   *oh right*

J   in the morning because your breakfast time is *sort of . . . um . . . well . . . oh . . .*   INFO. *J hesitates as she tries to find the breakfast time on her role sheet.*

T   what time?

J   you say the hotel doesn't serve the breakfast before half past seven

T   yeah

J   but I'm in a hurry now *I've got to leave by seven o'clock* so I couldn't have any breakfast   INFO. *No. It is already 7.00 a.m.*

T   OK

J   and that's . . . the other one is . . . the other reason is I couldn't have a bath in the morning because the water is cold

T   why . . . why the water is cold ah yeah

J   yeah the shower was cold

T   yeah hot water is . . . just available only after 7 a.m.

J   yeah but I only had cold water I couldn't have a bath so I just think it's *a bit funny* that I have to pay £30 £32 for the room with a bath including breakfast   LANG. *Not strong enough: 'unfair', 'unacceptable', 'ridiculous'.*

T *right right but the breakfast have been already included when you pay before so we couldn't pay it back* sorry

INFO. *Incorrect. The guest has not yet paid her bill.*

J yeah so I just thinking can you . . . *I just would like to reduce the price*

LANG. *'I would like you to reduce . . .'*

T yeah yeah

J so what do you think

T so

J because

T so I say like . . . I couldn't . . . no I can't do that

J yeah but the reason why I am asking you is in my room there is a price list they said . . . *the price for the room without bath is only 22 so I would like*

T *you mean*

J *to pay 22*

T *no it's 25*

J *oh yeah 25 that's right it's £25*

T *yeah*

INFO./COMM. *Guest gets the price wrong, but the two players deal effectively with that hitch.*

J so I would like to pay that £25 instead of 32 because I think that one is quite reasonable

T yes

J without bath

T but actually . . . the single room without bath and shower are cheaper because they are very small and don't have a *view* . . . so that's why the single room without bath shower are cheaper

LANG. *We think that T's pronunciation of the 'view' /bju:/ for /vju:/ makes it impossible for J to understand him. She gives no indication that she has taken his point.*

J yeah so

T actually your room has bath and shower

J but I couldn't have a bath because the hotel's condition was really bad

T yeah but actually you had a nice view from the window through the window and quite a nice wide room . . . yeah

J but from

T OK if you would like to see the single room without bath

J yeah

T do you want to see?

J but no I'm in hurry . . . I've got to leave now because I'm in a hurry I've got to go to London

T OK

J so I just would like to pay £25

T £25

J for the room without bath and that's the . . . really I didn't have a bath

T no

J and also I didn't have breakfast

T oh yeah but a single room with bath is more expensive because it has a nice view . . . a nice bed . . . actually . . . *a lot of sunshine* . . . a lot of windows . . . so that's why

STRAT. *Weak argument, which J could have attacked. Since she arrived late the night before and is leaving early today, sunshine is irrelevant to her case!*

J but I pay more money I wanted for good conditions but if I can't get good conditions so I think I wouldn't like to pay for that extra money

T right

J don't you think it's fair?

T *OK . . . so . . . OK I will pay back about only*
   shower OK? so it's just £2
J only £2?
T only £2
J for the shower?
T for the shower
J even I didn't have a shower?
T yeah
J well OK yeah thank you
T it's OK?
J thank you very much
T right not at all

STRAT. *Who gains more from this offer?*

(4½ minutes)

Afterwards, both players were reasonably satisfied with what they had achieved in the scenario. The guest had established the principle that she should be given some sort of refund; the assistant manager had managed to get all but £2 of the normal price for the room. In terms of language and communication, we also judged it a successful performance; minor breakdowns did occur, but they were dealt with effectively. There were no obvious signs that either player was unable to express their intended meaning.

SEMINAR SKILLS

The presentation recorded here is one from the speaking task in Unit 2, in which the students are asked to prepare a talk about the procedure for university entrance in their country. The speaker, Mihai, is Romanian.

Transcript 4

in Romania there is only one condition for being allowed to try to obtain a university place and this condition is to pass your school-leaving exam
   now what is the school-leaving exam? / to be clear in Romania we have the so-called general school also called elementary school which is eight years / and after that we have the high school which can be two years or four years / and to pass to give your school-leaving exam you have to do four years of high school / and . . . actually it's not very hard to pass this school-leaving exam because at least until now it was rather formal / and so you . . . it was very easy to be allowed to try entrance at any university you want because in spite of the fact that there is a large range of high schools in Romania / after you pass the school-leaving exam you can try to enter any university you want / it doesn't affect your choice
   and now *which* is the procedure of entrance? / almost in all the cases the entrance is / made on the basis of some written tests / and these written tests are in the subjects related with your choice / this . . . the number of the written tests can be two or three / for example in mathematics you have to write tests only in mathematical . . . subjects / algebra geometry

Not clear that Mihai is discussing a two-stage process: passing the school-leaving exam allows you to take the entrance exam.
Could have made clearer that he is opening a section of his talk with a question. Better to mark the question, e.g. 'The first question is . . .', and also to make a longer pause after the initial question.

= *what (because not a limited set)*

and *analysis* / in medicine you have to . . . you are
tested in physics biology and chemistry and so on /
some *sections* request preliminary examination / for
example architecture or music or fine arts / you have
to be tested in the specific skills which are needed for
it

   so the procedure is not very hard to understand it's
quite simple / and *there are some final notices* about
this procedure / for example the boys and the girls
don't compete each other / because the boys will go
into the army / and they will start the university one
year later

= *calculus*

= *faculties (departments)*

Better: 'I'd like to make one or two final comments.'
'There are' suggests a fixed agenda; 'notices' is
inappropriate.

(3 minutes)

Given our comments on Mihai's talk, our advice to him would be to mark the
sections more clearly and perhaps to speak a little slower. At times we felt that
non-native listeners in his audience would have had difficulty catching what he said.
We would also draw his attention to the various vocabulary points noted above and
to the fact that a simple visual aid would have made the presentation more
listener-friendly.

Bibliography

Anderson, A. and Lynch, T. (1988). *Listening*. Oxford: Oxford University Press.

Brown, G., Anderson, A., Shillcock, R. and Yule, G. (1984). *Teaching Talk*. Cambridge: Cambridge University Press.

Brown, G. and Yule, G. (1983). *Teaching the Spoken Language*. Cambridge: Cambridge University Press.

Bygate, M. (1987). *Speaking*. Oxford: Oxford University Press.

Bygate, M. (1988). Units of oral expression and language learning in small group interaction. *Applied Linguistics*, **9**/1: 59–82.

Canale, M. and Swain, M. (1980). Theoretical bases of communicative approaches to second language teaching and testing. *Applied Linguistics*, **1**/1: 1–47.

Corder, S.P. (1981). *Error Analysis and Interlanguage*. Oxford: Oxford University Press.

Di Pietro, R. (1987). *Strategic Interaction*. Cambridge: Cambridge University Press.

Dörnyei, Z. and Thurrell, S. (1991). Strategic competence and how to teach it. *English Language Teaching Journal*, **45**/1: 16–23.

Doughty, C. and Pica, T. (1986). 'Information gap' tasks: Do they facilitate second language acquisition? *TESOL Quarterly*, **20**/2: 305–25.

Duff, P. (1986). Another look at interlanguage talk: taking task to task. In R.R. Day (ed.), *Talking to Learn: Conversation in Second Language Acquisition*. Rowley, Mass: Newbury House.

Faerch, C. and Kasper, G. (1986). The role of comprehension in second language learning. *Applied Linguistics*, **7**/3: 257–74.

Krashen, S. (1981). *Second Language Acquisition and Second Language Learning*. Oxford: Pergamon.

Lynch, T. (1983*a*). Jigsaw speaking. *Modern English Teaching*, **11**/2: 34–38.

Lynch, T. (1983*b*). *Study Listening*. Cambridge: Cambridge University Press.

Lynch, T. and Anderson, K. (1989). 'Do you mind if I come in here?': a comparison of EAP materials and real seminars. Paper presented at the BALEAP Conference on Socio-Cultural Issues in Language Learning, Leeds, March 1989.

Mortimer, C. (1976). *Elements of Pronunciation*. Cambridge: Cambridge University Press.

Pica, T. and Doughty, C. (1985). The role of groupwork in classroom second language acquisition. *Studies in Second Language Acquisition*, **7**/1: 233–48.

Rutherford, W. (1987). *Second Language Grammar*. London: Longman.

Sharwood Smith, M. (1981). Consciousness-raising and the second language learner. *Applied Linguistics*, **2**/2: 159–68.

Swain, M. (1985). Communicative competence: some roles of comprehensible input and comprehensible output in its development. In S. Gass and C. Madden (eds), *Input in Second Language Acquisition*. Rowley, Mass: Newbury House.

Tarone, E. and Yule, G. (1989). *Focus on the Language Learner*. Oxford: Oxford University Press.

Ur, P. (1981). *Discussions that Work*. Cambridge: Cambridge University Press.